Tiger 131

The Epic Battle for Gueriat Ridge, Tunisia, 23-24 April 1943

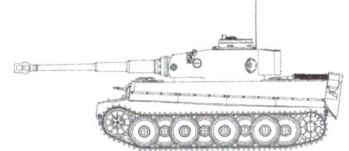

Tiger 131: The Epic Battle for Gueriat Ridge, Tunisia, 23-24 April 1943

by Bruce Oliver Newsome, Ph.D.
www.BruceNewsome.com

Find bonus chapters, photographs, and videos at:
www.patreon.com/bruceolivernewsome

Published by: Tank Archives Press, PO Box 181802, Coronado, California 92178, United States of America

Copyright © 2025 Tank Archives Press

All rights reserved. No part of this publication may be reproduced or stored in a retrieval system or transmitted, in any form or by any means, electronic, mechanical, photocopying, recording or otherwise, without prior permission in writing from Tank Archives Press.

HIS027100	HISTORY / Military / World War II
HIS027240	HISTORY / Military / Vehicles
POL036000	POLITICAL SCIENCE / Intelligence
NHWR7	Second World War
NHWL	Modern warfare
JWMV	Military vehicles
JWKF	Military Intelligence

ISBN: 978-1-951171-27-8

Acknowledgements

The author wishes to thank:

- Colin Alford, Canadian Armed Forces
- Niall Barr, Professor of Military History, Joint Services Command and Staff College, United Kingdom
- Rob Cogan, Curator, US Armor and Cavalry Collection
- John Dethlefsen, interned researcher
- David Fletcher, Historian, Tank Museum
- Jonathan Holt, Archives Assistant, Tank Museum
- Lauren Hunt, interned publishing assistant
- William Kang, interned market researcher
- Ian Mitchell, independent historian
- Dale Oscroft, independent historian
- R. Daniel Pellerin, Department of National Defence, Canada
- David Robertson, Ministry of Defence, United Kingdom
- Sheldon Rogers, Archives Assistant, Tank Museum
- Audrey Sherev, interned copy-editor
- Katie Thompson, Archives Assistant, Tank Museum
- Stuart Wheeler, Archives Manager, Tank Museum
- Edward Wicks, Foreign and Commonwealth Office, United Kingdom
- David Willey, Curator, Tank Museum

All photographs are courtesy of the Bundesarchiv (Germany), US Army Center for Military History, National Archives (US), Imperial War Museum, Tank Museum (Britain), David Robertson, Alan Wilson, and Bruce Oliver Newsome.

CONTENTS

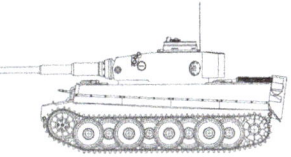

Abbreviations	4
Introduction	5
Map	6
Chapter 1: Tiger 131's Day of Triumph	**7**
Forces	7
Point 101	7
Point 158	8
The gulley in between	8
Point 174	8
The new attack on Point 174	10
Point 144	10
Enter the Tiger	10
Point 158 abandoned	11
Tiger triumphant	13
Outcomes	14
Chapter 2: The Second Day	**15**
Forces	15
Plans	15
Point 158	17
Point 151	17
Point 174	19
Chapter 3: Tiger 131 Versus Infantry	**21**
Defensive positions	21
The German counter-attacks	21
Tiger 131's counter-attack	21
Tiger 131 versus a PIAT	24
Tiger 131 versus a towed 75-mm gun	24
Chapter 4: Tiger 131 Versus Shell Fire	**25**
External damage	25
Turret traverse	25
Gun elevation and depression	28
Internal fittings	28
Tiger 131 versus machine-guns	28
Chapter 5: Tiger 131 Versus Churchill Tanks	**33**
Point 151	33
Point 144	33
Tiger 131's demise	34
The lifting boss	34
Under the armament	35
Damage to the turret traverse	38
Loader's hatch	38
Commander's cupola	39
Chapter 6: Churchills on Point 174	**41**
From Point 144	41
More reported Panzers	41
Distant fire	42
In the gulley	43
Point 174 again	43
Withdrawal	44
Outcomes	45
Chapter 7: The Consolidation of Point 174	**47**
The day after	47
The second day after	48
The remaining days on Point 174	48
Escalating Tiger 131	49
Recovering Tiger 131	49
References	51
Index	53

ABBREVIATIONS

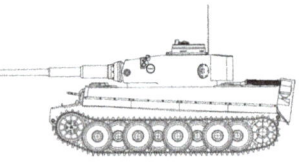

ACIGS	Assistant Chief of the Imperial General Staff
AB	armoured brigade
AD	armoured division
AFHQ	Allied Force Headquarters
AFV	armoured fighting vehicle
a.k.a.	also known as
amn	ammunition
AP	armour-piercing; Associated Press
APC	armour-piercing, capped
APCBC	armour-piercing, capped, ballistic capped
APCR	armour-piercing, composite rigid
APDS	armour-piercing, discarding sabot
API	armour-piercing, incendiary
APT	armour-piercing, tracer
AT	anti-tank
Ausf.	*Ausführung* (mark or iteration)
bhp	brake horse-power
BAOR	British Army of the Rhine
BRAC	Brigader Royal Armoured Corps
CC	Combat Command
CIGS	Chief of the Imperial General Staff
CIOS	Combined Intelligence Objectives Sub-Committee
cm	centimetres
CP	command post
CT	Combat Team
DADME	Deputy Assistant Director of Mechanical Engineering
DAFV	Directorate of Armoured Fighting Vehicles
DCIGS	Deputy Chief of the Imperial General Staff
DDAFV(T)	Deputy Director Armoured Fighting Vehicles Technolog
DDGA	Deputy Director-General of Artillery
DDME	Deputy Director of Mechanical Engineering
DGA	Director-General of Artillery
DGAE	Director-General for Army Equipment
dm	decimetres
DME	Director of Mechanical Engineering
DMI	Directorate of Military Intelligence
DMO&I	Directorate of Military Operations and Intelligence
DRA	Director Royal Artillery
DRAC	Director Royal Armoured Corps
DTD	Department of Tank Design
DW	*Durchbruchswagen* (breakthrough vehicle)
FA	Field Artillery
FlaK	*Fliegerabwehrkanone* (anti-aircraft gun)
FO	(British) Foreign Office
fps	feet per second
ft.	feet
FVPE	(British) Fighting Vehicle Proving Establishment
G1	(American) staff responsible for personnel
G2	(American) staff responsible for intelligence
G3	(American) staff responsible for operations and training
G4	(American) staff responsible for logistics
GC&CS	(British) Government Code and Cypher School
GHQ	General Headquarters (usually army or regional echelor
HC	hollow charge (shaped charge)
HE	high-explosive
HEAT	high-explosive anti-tank (HC)
HET	high-explosive, tracer
hp	horse-power
HQ	headquarters
hrs.	hours (24-hour clock)
IC	in charge
in.	inch
IWM	Imperial War Museum
JIC	(British) Joint Intelligence Comittee
km	kilometres
kmh	kilometres per hour
KwK	*Kampfwagenkanone* (fighting vehicle gun)
L	length in calibres
lb.	pound
m	metres
M	model
MC	military cross
MEC	Middle East Command
MEW	Ministry for Economic Warfare
MG	machine-gun
MI	military intelligence
Mk.	mark
mm	millimetres
MP	Member of Parliament; Military Police
mph	miles per hour
MQ	machineable quality armour (also: RHA)
m/s	metres per second
OKW	*Oberkommando der Wehrmacht* (High Command)
OR	other rank
OSS	(United States) Office of Strategic Services
PaK	*Panzerabwehrkanone* (anti-tank gun)
Panzer	*Panzerkampfwagen* (armoured fighting vehicle)
pdr	pounder
Pkw	*Personenkraftwagen* (personnel carrier)
Pz.Kfw.	*Panzerkampfwagen* (armoured fighting vehicle)
Pz.Kw.	*Panzerkampfwagen* (armoured fighting vehicle)
pr	pounder (see: pdr)
QF	quick firing
RA	Royal Artillery
RAC	Royal Armoured Corps
RE	Royal Engineers
REME	Royal Electrical and Mechanical Engineers
RHA	rolled homogenous armour; Royal Horse Artillery
RTR	Royal Tank Regiment
Sd.Kfz.	*Sonderkraftfahrzeug* (special purpose vehicle)
SHAEF	Supreme Headquarters Allied Expeditionary Force
SIS	(British) Secret Intelligence Service (MI6)
s.Pz.Abt.	*schwere Panzer Abteilung* (heavy tank battalion)
sq.	square
SS	steamship; *Schutzstaffel* (protection staff)
StuG	*Sturmgeschütz* (assault vehicle)
StuK	*Sturmgeschützkanone* (assault vehicle gun)
STT	School of Tank Technology
SW	*Sturmwagen* (assault vehicle)
TCV	troop-carrying vehicle
TD	Tank Destroyer
tk.	tank
TM	The Tank Museum, Bovington
TNT	trinitrotoluene (explosive)
UK	United Kingdom
UP	United Press
US(A)	United States (of America)
WD	War Department
WO	War Office
WTSFF	Weapons Technical Staff Field Force
yds.	yards

INTRODUCTION

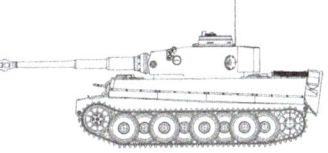

Tiger 131 of the 504th Heavy Tank Battalion is the first running Tiger to be exploited by Western intelligence, the most studied Tiger, and the only Tiger running today.

Its capture in late April 1943 was the climax to more than four months of fighting between German Tiger tanks and Western Allied forces in Tunisia.

The Allies didn't even know they were fighting Tigers in December 1942.

They first captured a Tiger in late January. This was Tiger 231 of the 501st Heavy Tank Battalion. But it was holed and burning. Within hours of its disablement inside Allied lines, the Germans recaptured it, long enough to demolish it (Newsome 2020c).

For two calendar months, the wreck of Tiger 231 remained the only Tiger in Western Allied territory…

…until seven demolished Tigers fell into British hands in early March, at Hunts Gap. Seven sounds like a great quantity…but these wrecks were not as revealing as Tiger 231 had been (Newsome 2020d).

Most of April passed without further technical intelligence.

On 21 April, a single Tiger held off the British at Djebel Djaffa, until the Germans strangely abandoned it overnight. Yet the British forgot about Tiger 712 in their hurry to launch their great offensive, as scheduled, on the next day (the 22nd of April).

Towards the end of that day, the British knocked out Tiger 731, towards the southern end of the offensive.

However, they could not exploit Tiger 731 safely while Axis forces retained the dominant heights.

Trumping all these trophies was Tiger 131 of the 504th, abandoned, in almost perfect condition, atop Gueriat Ridge, astride a road to Tunis, on 24th April. Yet Tiger 131's provenance came to be lost in a false claim by Peter Gudgin that Tiger 131 was the same Tiger that had been found abandoned below Djebel Djaffa two days earlier (i.e., Tiger 712). He had fought Tiger 712, but not Tiger 131. Nevertheless, years later, Gudgin persuaded the Tank Museum to adjust the place and date of capture. The errors were not corrected until a few years ago (Newsome 2020e).

While the discourse obsessed with the where and when, everybody forgot to explain the battles on and around Gueriat Ridge. These battles remained untold until I was invited to examine Tiger 131 in 2019, for clues as to how Tiger 131 was defeated, captured, recovered, diassembled, and restored. From there, I researched the archives in Britain and Germany, and the battlefields in Tunisia, and pieced together the battles that had been forgotten.

The battles for Gueriat Ridge are much greater in scale, space, and forces – and heroism – than would be suggested by the well-worn photographs of Tiger 131, sitting alone on a hill top, after capture.

My research identified eight hill tops at issue when the British attacked on 23rd April. These hills were parts of an Axis defensive line that the Allies hoped to break through, all the way to Tunis. Tiger 131 was able to influence all the hills from Gueriat Ridge. Amazingly, it fought for two days, against parts of four battalions of tanks and six battalions of infantry.

Tiger 131 was probably the only German tank fighting on Gueriat Ridge from 23 to 24 April…

Each day, it faced about 50 Churchill tanks. Tiger 131's superior lethality and survivability, and tactics, kept most of these tanks in hiding or on difficult approaches. where most broke down or ditched. Additionally, Tiger 131 knocked out around five Churchills each day.

It was an impressive performance. It deserves to be remembered as one of the greatest defenses by a single tank.

As I explain, a combination of weapons, and accumulated damage (some of it preceding the battles for Gueriat Ridge), provoked German abandonment of Tiger 131. Its defeat proved decisive to British victory there.

This book examines the evidence and theories, and reconstructs the fights, using exhaustive forensic examination of Tiger 131 itself, the archives, and the battlefields.

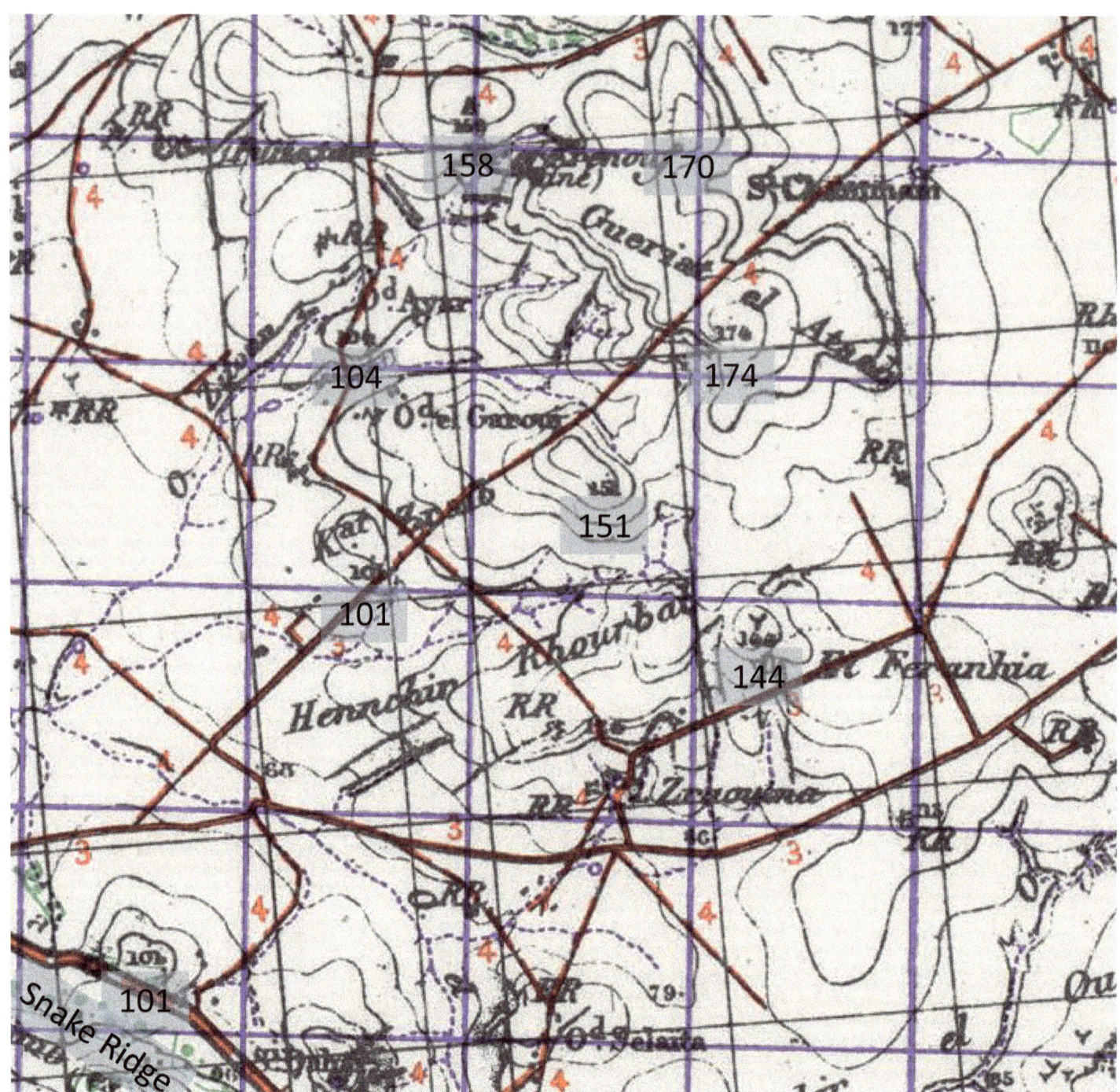

This map shows eight of the summits at issue on 23rd April. Most Allied approaches came around Snake Ridge and Point 101, north-westwards to a separate Point 101 ("Kat Zralb"), then in three directions: north across Point 104 to Point 158 (also reported as 156), then east to Point 170 (also reported as 176); north-eastwards across Point 151 to Point 174; and south-eastwards to Point 144. The war diaries and reports betray the participants' confusion about these hills. Typically, they conflate all objectives to Point 174, which is the tallest, or "Guerriat Ridge," which includes only two or three summits. They tended to approach "Snake Ridge" from around the western end of "Banana Ridge," and to refer to the battlefield as "Banana Ridge." This could be confused with Gueriat el Atach, which is shaped like a banana (its apex points towards the attackers). Other units referred to "Medjez el Bab," which is more than 7 miles (11.5 km) to the west-south-west of Point 174. "Medjez el Bab" is the title of the map sheet, covering nearly 600 square km (230 square miles): this cutting shows about 25 square km (10 square miles). The sheet is based on a French map from 1935, which proved fuzzy when facsimiled, even in greyscale: the colour overlays are British; each blue square represents a square km. The northern boundary of the sheet is the same in this cutting. The connecting sheet to the north used different symbology, so was difficult to line up. On the connecting sheet, just to the north of Point 158, was Point 168, which was another objective, but not captured for days. Also on the connecting sheet was the hamlet of Montarnaud, about 3,000 yards (2,700 m) north-east from Point 174: the Germans used it as a hub for their responses, until it was captured in the final Allied offensive, on 6th May. In the 1970s, Peter Gudgin claimed that 48th RTR knocked out Tiger 131 on 21st April, on Djebel Djaffa, 10 miles (16 km) to south-west (Newsome 2020d).

CHAPTER 1

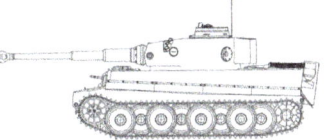

TIGER 131's DAY OF TRIUMPH

On 23rd April 1943, while Tiger 731 was being defeated by British IX Corps (see Newsome 2020d), the 1st Infantry Division of V Corps attacked the hills between the Medjerda river and the Medjez-Tunis highway. The Germans had developed a defensive line here since capturing these hills on 10th December 1942 (see Newsome 2020c). After two days of fighting, Tiger 131 was captured, although the hills remained contested.

Forces

Overnight, 22nd-23rd April, British patrols confirmed that Snake Ridge and Point 101, astride the highway from Tunis to Medjez-el-Bab (see Map) were clear of enemy. The 2nd Infantry Brigade, supported by Churchill tanks, started from Snake Ridge to capture seven other summits overlooking the highway. The terrain was complex, even by the standards of Northern Tunisia. Allied mapping had not improved significantly since the area had been lost 4.5 months earlier; and intelligence on the defensive line did not specify much more than the formations.

The British corps boundary was practically the same as the German divisional boundary. The area north of the Medjez-Tunis highway (all the way across the river to Chouigui, nearly 15.5 miles (28 km) from Point 174), was held by German 334th Division. The area south of the highway was held by the incomplete Hermann Göring Division. Allied intelligence estimated three infantry battalions on 2nd Infantry Brigade's objectives, excluding an infantry battalion in reserve, with some Panzers. In fact, these forces were defending a longer front that included the hills to the northwest, which were already under attack by 78th Division and the 24th Guards Brigade (which was advancing between 1st Division and 78th Division). Lieutenant-General C.W. Allfrey (V Corps) had commanded this area since November: he visited the units involved on 22nd April, to explain that the operation should demolish the final German defensive line before a victorious breakthrough to Tunis.

The 2nd Brigade committed all three battalions: they were eventually reinforced or replaced with all three battalions from 3rd Brigade. Both brigades came from 1st Division, which was inexperienced except with defensive duties. One battalion of Churchill tanks (142nd RAC) was committed on the first day, followed by a composite battalion made up from three tank battalions (142nd RAC; 145th RAC; 48th RTR), from both of the tank brigades (25TB and 21TB) in Tunisia. Each battalion was authorized with 58 Churchill tanks and 10 M3 Lights or Bren Gun Carriers for reconnaissance, although each had been decimated in the preceding days of fighting.

According to German unit reports, perhaps 10 Tigers were operational on 23rd April, of an inventory of around 15. Tigers made up half to three-quarters of all surviving Panzers in Tunisia. Tiger 131 is the only German tank that can be identified in this battle, even though at least nine different Allied tankies or infantrymen claimed to strike a tank on Point 174. The 142nd RAC produced at least four claims to knock out tanks on Point 174 on the first day, including at least one Tiger, but none was found when it returned on the second day. On that second day, Churchill tanks on four separate hills claimed to fight a tank on Point 174, while the infantry produced their own claim, but Tiger 131 was the only German tank found. It shows only two strikes from AP shots. Probably, Tiger 131 was the only German tank to fight on Point 174, although towed guns and dummy tanks provided the illusion of other Tigers.

Point 101

Starting from Snake Ridge, the 1st Battalion, Loyal Regiment (North Lancashire), was on the left, heading for Point 104, Point 158, and Point 170; the 2nd North Staffordshires were in the middle, heading over Point 151 to Point 174; and the 1st Gordon Highlanders were on the right, aiming for Point 144. All three battalions started at 0200 hours, 23rd April. A creeping barrage started at 0230 hours in front of the Staffordshires and Gordons, and at 0300 hours in front of the Loyals. Altogether, five field artillery units (120 25-pounders), one medium unit (16 4.5-inch howitzers), and four heavy batteries (32 5.5-inch howitzers) were allocated. The high-explosive shells would create terrific dust and smoke in the dry elevated areas, which mixed with obfuscatory smoke (five percent of shells) to blind attackers and defenders alike.

One squadron of tanks from 142nd RAC was supposed to reached Point 158 and Point 174 respectively by dawn (0530 hours). The C Squadron stayed on Point 101, just north of the highway (bottom left corner of the map), but within range of mortars, which killed two crewmen and wounded a motorcyclist from A Echelon (ammunition and fuel).

The A and B Squadrons crossed the highway at 0200 hours but took until 0445 hours to cover the 5 miles (8 km) to the other Point 101 (Kat Zralb). Several tanks shed tracks, "owing to the roughness of the path," according to the war diary. The unit HQ occupied the farm buildings just to the south-west.

Point 158

Starting at dawn (0530 hours), the A Squadron had headed north up the track for about 2,200 yards (2,000 m) to Point 158 (a round hill just beyond the north-western end of "Gueriat el Atach"). Only 7 of its nominal 18 tanks had got to Kat Zralb. At the foot of Point 158, two tanks were disabled on mines. A separate tank was perforated by a shot that killed the driver and carried away a leg of the artillery's Forward Observation Officer, who was riding in the turret. The remaining four tanks occupied the summit, while the 1st Loyals caught up.

The Loyals had started from the highway on a front of just 600 yards, with six platoons forward – two from the D Company (on the left), two from A Company (in the middle), and two from B Company (on the right). The battalion's forward HQ was following; the C Company was keeping the rear. The support company remained behind Banana Ridge, until 0300 hours. At Kat Zralb, they could spread out. Indeed, from here the Loyals faced the widest front of the three battalions and the furthest objectives, but was not given any exceptional support.

On the left, the D Company struggled most. It was supposed to keep the north-bound track on its left, gain Point 158, and even gain Point 168, which is 1,200 yards (1,100 m) north of Point 174. Short of Point 158, six machine-guns and a mortar stopped the company. Two subalterns were mortally wounded.

The gulley in between

On the right, the B Company found its way by keeping its right flank in sight of the track running across Point 151 and Point 174. It crossed the rise on the other side of the track to Point 151, then descended into the gulley. By keeping close to the barrage, and by the good fortune of passing between German positions, it gained the reverse slope to the north-west of Point 174 by 0400 hours, with one dead and six wounded, and sixteen German prisoners.

In the middle, the A Company captured an enemy patrol without fighting, but 200 yards further on was stopped by enemy machine-guns and mortars. The company eventually cleared the enemy position and took 40 prisoners, but had fallen behind the barrage. More machine-guns and mortars opened up from the area traversed by B Company, then four men detonated landmines. The A Company backtracked. It tried to get to the right of the enemy, then to the left, before erring rightwards to the track. By 0500 hours, it had crossed the gulley and was abreast of Point 174. From the crest, it tried to reach Point 170, with supporting fire from the rightmost platoon of D Company, but was suppressed. At 0600 hours, it tried again: only Lieutenant D.B. Carter and two other men got to the summit, then were driven off by mortars. They must have settled on the reverse slope towards the middle of the ridge, but the accounts are unclear.

The battalion's forward HQ was following A Company, but lost touch, and followed its own compass bearing over a gulley (probably aiming for the nose-shaped feature on the map, below the "G" of "Gueriat el Atach"). About 0315 hours, Lieutenant-Colonel G.W. Gibson was mortally wounded by a landmine. Major H.D. Oclee went to his assistance, but suffered the same fate. The intelligence sergeant too was killed. Only three remained (the adjutant, the intelligence officer, and the wireless operator). They tended to the wounded, then the adjutant (Captain J.A. Hamilton) evacuated across the gulley into a field of wheat, where C Company was waiting (probably around "Od. El Garour" on the map). Gibson was heard calling for help, so the intelligence officer (Lieutenant E.W. Hawkins) and a volunteer went back with a stretcher to bring him back. During the move, Hawkins tripped a mine that wounded his leg. Gibson had been left behind, by some misunderstanding, but the battalion's medical officer went to attend.

Major G.A. Bouch of C Company assumed command of the battalion. Given machine-gun fire across the ridge, he withdrew to dead ground near Point 104, by 0415 hours. The Allied barrage had ceased at 0410 hours, then enemy mortaring increased on all the forward troops, while enemy infantry infiltrated the wheatfield to snipe on Battalion HQ. The support company came up on schedule, so Bouch placed it in reserve. Then he sent the C Company to help D Company, which was the only company he could contact by radio. However, both were pinned by machine-guns and mortars and soon needed ammunition. The carrier platoon resupplied them twice, but its commander was wounded on the third attempt. Around then, the A Squadron's four remaining tanks got up to Point 158, followed by the C Company. Soon thereafter, about 50 Scots Guards, without officers, drifted in from 24th Guards Brigade on the left (north) flank. This was sometime before 0700 hours, when the Universal Carriers withdrew to fetch more ammunition: one carrier broke its track, and two crewmen were killed fixing it.

Point 174

Meanwhile, the 2nd North Staffordshires were on Point 174. The two leading companies had climbed Point 151 with little difficulty, by 0300 hours, but on the crest ran into barbed wire, landmines, and machine-gun fire. After a steep descent into the gulley, and up the other side, they occupied Point 174 at 0400 hours. The second company lost contact in the smoke, and mistakenly advanced beyond, where it was counter-attacked at 0500 hours. The wheat was mature on that side of the hill, so the British were forced to stand to return fire. This company fell back on Point 174, with its ammunition almost exhausted. The Staffords had lost communications with other arms, so had no idea where the tanks were (Cook, 1970, p. 110).

The 142nd RAC war diary took no responsibility, but recorded that its liaison officer with the infantry was wounded at some point. The B Squadron was in support of the Staffordshires: it was supposed to cross the "Kat Zralb" junction at dawn (0530 hours), but did not arrive in time to see the second German counter-attack. Now, the Germans focused on B Company of the Loyals, to the north-west of the track, at 0615 hours. Six armoured cars supported infantry in overrunning the forward sections. By 0645 hours, a German machine-gun was established near Point 174, from where it harassed B Company, whose mortar attachment responded. It was at this point that B Company noticed seven Churchill tanks on the reverse slope of Point 174. The 142nd RAC's war diary claimed to support the infantry back on to the hill, which probably means that the tankies encouraged stragglers in the gulley. Getting to the crest of Hill 174, the surviving tanks took hull-down positions astride the track. Two Churchills were knocked out by alleged anti-tank guns on the other side, with the loss of one killed and one wounded. Two more were "rendered immobile," perhaps by land-mines rather than the anti-tank guns, but continued to fire.

At 0700 hours, the Germans stormed Point 174 again, and shattered all three companies of the Staffords. Survivors fled to Hill 151, where the reserve company was located. By 0930 hours, the Germans had driven off the A and B Companies of the Loyals too: they made their way back to their Battalion HQ near Point 104.

Lieutenant Wilward A. Sandys-Clark was the only remaining officer with B Company. Although wounded in neck and head by splinters, he convinced the unit's third commander of the morning (Major E. Fulbrook had taken over at 0545 hours, having obtained permission from 2nd Brigade to give up his duties as route controller) that he could retake B Company's objective with about 20 men. After good progress, they were pinned by a machine-gun. He arranged for the men to give covering fire, then charged in with a revolver, killing or capturing the crew. However, two other machine-guns opened fire soon thereafter. Sandys-Clarke sensibly reported by radio that he could go no further. Fulbrook replied, "Try battle-drill tactics." Sandys-Clarke arranged for covering fire, then charged alone again, putting both guns out of action. Thence he led the men to the objective. Shortly before midday, he was still consolidating the position, when two snipers opened fire. Sandys-Clarke went forward alone, but was killed a few feet from a sniper. He was awarded a Victoria Cross posthumously.

These fragments of HE shells were collected from Point 151 in 2019. Their nationality is impossible to identify. They came from the British creeping barrage or the German defensive fire.

This German anti-personnel mine (cement with metal fragments) was found in 2019 on the top of Point 151.

The new attack on Point 174

Sometime after the Staffords failed, Brigadier Eric Moore of the 2nd Brigade committed his reserve (the 1st Duke of Wellington's Regiment, detached from 3rd Brigade). This battalion needed to come from behind Banana Ridge to the second Point 101 (Kat Zralb), from where Point 174 was easily identified by a blazing Churchill tank. The commander (Lieutenant-Colonel Brian Webb-Carter) and adjutant arrived first in a Universal Carrier. They were met by Moore, who ordered them to relieve both the Loyals and the Staffordshires. This meant distributing a company on each of Point 158, Point 151, and Point 174. Webb-Carter conferred with the acting commander of the Staffordshires, who confirmed that no infantry were on Point 174. Then the commander of 142nd RAC (A.E. Birkbeck) took him to Point 151 in a Churchill tank. They could see two or three Churchills below the crest of Point 174, but no other British forces.

Returning to Kat Zralb, Webb-Carter found his B Company just arrived: he ordered it on to Point 174 at once, and ordered C and D Companies to follow as soon as possible. The 142nd RAC re-committed its B Squadron, and timed the attack at 1300 hours. Their advance was dive-bombed, although with few casualties. On the reverse slope of Point 174, the B Company was pinned by German fire from the crest. Two FOOs were killed trying to observe forward.

Point 144

The 2nd Brigade's third and final battalion (1st Gordon Highlanders) was on Point 144 – 1,000 yards (900 m) southeast of Point 151, and 1,600 yards (1,500 m) south of Point 174. This battalion got on to its objective before dawn, with little opposition, and without tanks, although 12 were killed or wounded. Twenty Germans surrendered. The Gordon Highlanders had been carrying rations and ammunition sufficient for days of fighting, and anti-personnel mines for their defensive perimeter; the battalion's Universal Carriers delivered tools and more ammunition. The Gordons were frequently under indirect fire, and received a counter-attack that was discouraged by close fire, principally on the left-most company (A Company). On the right, B Company were withdrawn slightly early in the afternoon to escape particularly severe indirect fire. The other two companies were to the west (Miles, 1961, p. 175-177).

At 1330 hours, the 142nd RAC's liaison officer there reported tanks approaching from the south-east. These tanks presumably had been called from reserve along the highway to Tunis, which runs south-westwards to as close as 3,600 yards (3,300 m) from Point 144. Birkbeck organized what he called a "perimeter defence": a composite troop from A Squadron, the squadron commander, and unit HQ were on Point 158; the Intelligence Officer's tank (probably a close-support tank; temporarily commanded by Lieutenant J.W. Salmons) was on the north-western corner of Point 158; B Squadron was on Point 174; and C Squadron was on the southern slope of Point 151. Two A Squadron tanks and three HQ tanks opened fire at long range on tanks approaching Point 158; the adjutant's tank claimed one certain hit.

At 1400 hours, Birkbeck recalled a composite troop from B Squadron and two troops from C Squadron to Kat Zralb, and ordered his second-in-command (Major S.D.G. Robertson) to lead them to Point 144. The B Squadron was left with one composite troop around Point 174, under the squadron's commander (Major F.G.L. Lyne). Presumably they had consolidated with the rump of C Squadron behind Point 151, because the war diary recorded none of its engagements after 1300 hours, despite an exceptionally detailed entry for the day.

Later, a troop of repaired tanks from A Squadron got on Point 144, where they were mortared and dive-bombed.

Enter the Tiger

Sometime between 1400 and 1600 hours, Robertson's tank broke a track, which had been weakened already by a landmine. Two crews were repairing this (the other crew was from the commander of one of C Squadron's troops – Lieutenant J.E. Forrest) when a tank appeared on Point 174. Robertson and Forrest identified this as a Panzer IV, but the Dukes on Point 174 and the rest of the 142nd RAC identified it as a Tiger. Forrest claimed "probably" to destroy it, before a shot carried away the first wheel unit on his left side: he reversed out of trouble. The other Churchills spent their time trying to engage enemy mortars from positions out of sight of the Tiger.

Meanwhile, the remainder of C Squadron, still on the south side of Point 151, claimed to knock out an anti-tank gun (in a wheatfield to the right of Point 174) and several tanks, including a Tiger taking cover behind one of B Squadron's knocked-out Churchills on the track near the crest of Point 174. The cover might have been a Churchill IV of 142nd RAC that was later located by 48th RTR's recovery team, at 25TB's request, "on last rise before Pt. 174, bellied with track off." The Dukes fled. Webb-Carter later wrote:

> About 1600 hours, after spasmodic dive-bombing and heavy mortaring, I was surprised to see some men of B Company walking back past Battalion Headquarters [presumably at Kat Zralb]. Asking what this was in aid of, one of the men said, "There's a Boche tank in our position."
>
> "Rubbish," I said, "Come back with me," and walked with them up to their position, when I was appalled to be confronted by an enormous Tiger tank. Our tanks had apparently withdrawn for some reason. I rushed to my wireless set and bleated to [2nd] Brigade about the Tiger and asked for some tanks. The only immediate reaction was that our positions were heavily shelled by our own artillery.

Tiger 131 takes a track between an olive grove and a meadow. Tiger 142 and at least one other Tiger of the 504th feature in the same series of photographs. Tiger 131 is differentiated by the step welded to the nose, and the hand-hold on the glacis. All the Tigers photographed in this series lack the binocular optics for the driver: the drilled apertures above his visor were filled with welds. Tiger 131 has already been damaged by high-explosive shells: the top-most smoke discharger on the turret's left side is missing; and the cupola, upper edge of the turret, mantlet, and driver's plate are scarred, particularly to the main armament's left and in its shadow. The date must be in April 1943: possibly Tiger 131 is deploying to Gueriat el Atach.

Around 1600 hours, the 142nd RAC recorded receipt of a message from 2nd Brigade HQ referring to an "incredible" number of enemy tanks approaching from the south-east. Somebody was miscommunicating. The 142nd RAC blamed 2nd Brigade HQ, which subsequent events seem to confirm.

At that time, 142nd RAC's commander was liaising with one of the infantry battalions, so the Adjutant recalled all tanks to Point 101, except to leave a composite troop from A Squadron around each of Point 158, Point 174, and Point 144. The remaining tanks were formed into a composite squadron, under Major F.W. Roper, who had come to Kat Zralb on orders to replenish the tanks. The composite squadron included four repaired tanks, of the 11-odd that had shed tracks during A Squadron's approach. Presumably the rest remained too hazardous to recover. At some point in the afternoon, one of the unit's two recovery tanks was recovering a Churchill (probably from A Squadron), when an enemy plane's machine-guns killed a crewman.

Point 158 abandoned

At 1130 hours, Captain G.B Wilson, who had taken over as brigade route controller once Fulbrook departed at 0545 hours, arrived to take over C Company of the Loyals, but was shortly wounded.

Around midday, 24th Guards Brigade, supported by 145th RAC, consolidated on a hill a mile to the north-west of Point 158. On this excuse, the four running tanks of A Squadron withdrew. Lieutenant A.H. Dodson and his crewmen stayed in their disabled tank, using its radio to pass on to the artillery the information that he was receiving (on foot) from the infantry, who were spotting targets on the other side of Point 158. At 1515 hours, he saw at least two tanks taking positions between Point 158 and Point 174 to the south-east. He was training the tank's gun when his tank was hit; his driver was killed evacuating. The four survivors eventually escaped back to unit HQ.

The Loyals' support company sent three six-pounder guns to Point 158, but around Point 104 one gun and its tractor (a Universal Carrier) were knocked out. The shots were attributed to an 88-mm gun, which must have been a Tiger tank, probably the same tank that killed Dodson's Churchill. The other two six-pounders withdrew into a gulley.

At 1600 hours, German tanks and infantry, supported by mortars, forced C Company to abandon Point 158. The 2nd Brigade HQ then ordered the 1st Loyals to defend a perimeter around the farm behind Kat Zralb.

(Left) According to the numbers assigned to these photographs in German archives, Tiger 131 was photographed on this highway before turning on to the track. On the highway, all the Tigers were camouflaged with branches, and carried crewmen externally, presumably to look out for enemy aircraft. However, on the track, the Tigers lacked camouflage or crewmen externally. Possibly, the crewmen did not want their vision devices obscured once they entered the battlefield. Alternatively, possibly the negatives were archived out of sequence, in which case the photographs on the track depict the Tigers leaving their assembly area, before adjusting to mitigate the risks of air attack on the highway.

(Right) The last photograph in the same series shows two Tigers descending a track away from the olive grove, possibly to their final assigned positions of the day. The series leaves no other clues to location or timing, although the date is likely in April, given the weather, terrain, and the damage to Tiger 131. The first three Tigers of the 504th had landed on 12th March, the eleventh Tiger on 16th April. The two photographs of Tiger 131 in this series are the only known photographs of Tiger 131 before capture.

Tiger triumphant

At 1800 hours, 2nd Brigade ordered 142nd RAC to support yet a fifth battalion (2nd Sherwood Foresters, detached from 3rd Brigade) on to Point 174, and to hold it at all costs. This meant making recalling the troops from Points 158, 174 and Point 144. Major Lyne's composite troop arrived from Point 174 without further harm, although Lyne was left out of battle to rally the crews. Perhaps he was considered too stressed to continue without a rest. Robertson's tank was still being repaired at 1800 hours, so Lieutenant C.V.K. Lister (a troop commander in C Squadron) took command of all the tanks on Point 144 and led its evacuation. However, his tank hit a landmine. Then his troop sergeant's tank hit a landmine. Forrest's tank caught up 30 minutes later (Churchills were capable of running without some of their 22 roadwheels), but also hit a landmine. Robertson started 10 minutes later, picked up Forrest's crew, and navigated the minefields successfully.

The 142nd RAC's intelligence officer had been sent to find the HQ of the Sherwood Foresters, but their commander said that the battalion was still six miles behind. By the time he got back to 142nd RAC HQ, the commander of 25TB was there: R.H. Maxwell took responsibility for telling 1ID HQ that no attack was feasible that day. However, after Maxwell had departed, 142nd RAC received orders to attack without infantry. Fourteen available tanks mustered around Kat Zralb, led by Roper. After seeing them off, the intelligence officer took a scout car back to find any other Churchills that had been made battleworthy.

Roper ordered his composite squadron to take the track up to Point 151 in column, then to fan out into line, to the left of the track, for an advance to the crest between Point 174 and Point 170. Although Roper issued the plan, Birkbeck decided to lead. Webb-Carter was with him.

> About half an hour later a squadron of our Churchills arrived, led by Lieut[enant]-Colonel Birkbeck, their commanding officer. He said to me, "Where is this Tiger?" I walked beside his tank up a small rise and immediately the Tiger made one of its periodic appearances. Birkbeck had his head out of his turret and peered through field-glasses at the Tiger. Poor devil! Just as he said, "Right; I've got it now," the Tiger fired its 88-mm gun and scored a direct hit on Birkbeck's Churchill. Birkbeck disappeared into the tank, which then brewed up. We pulled out the driver, who was badly burned, but Birkbeck was killed outright. This was too much for the tank squadron, who packed up and left us to get on with it. (Barclay, 1953, p. 54)

Birkbeck's tank was hit twice and set afire, killing everybody except the gunner. The 142nd RAC war diary describes the tanks approaching the crest in failing light, probably around dusk (1900 hours), where they received heavy fire, including 88-mm shots. One tank from B Squadron got stuck on a mound; another tank broke a track; both were left behind. Roper claimed to knock out a Tiger tank, Panzer IV, and Panzer III on Point 174, although none was found by the attackers the next day – perhaps he was firing on the six dummy tanks that would be identified on the other side of Point 174 two days later.

The rump A Squadron remained somewhere around Point 158, from where it claimed to engage enemy tanks and infantry during the final German counter-attack. It abandoned a tank after its commander was blinded by blood from a slight wound (caused by mortaring).

The engagements did not end until complete darkness, when Roper ordered his tanks to turn about and head left of Birkbeck's burning tank in order to find the track, then to follow the tracers fired by enemy machine-guns. These tracers were still flying over their heads as they were withdrawing over Point 151. One tank stayed there for an hour to fulfil a commitment to cover the withdrawal of the 1st Dukes.

Outcomes

The 142nd RAC's sixteen surviving tanks included just four from A Squadron, even though at least seven had been repaired and re-committed during the day. The sixteen leaguered in scrubland between Point 101 and Snake Ridge, until somebody realised that the same location had received indirect fire during the day. They moved at 0400 hours for 2,200 yards (2 km) westwards along the highway. By then, 12 tanks had been recovered to 104th Army Tank Workshop, for a further 8 miles (13 km), by highway through Medjez and along a secondary road to its south.

The war diary refers to 14 abandoned with broken tracks, bellied, or ditched, 7 disabled on landmines, and 6 hit by AP shots, one of which was counted as finished by a landmine. These add up to 26. Adding the 12 recovered earlier to workshops, plus the 16 surviving tanks, gets us to 54 tanks. This total leaves 4 tanks unaccounted, of the 58 authorized to the unit. Perhaps these four are those nominally assigned to the battalion HQ. Alternatively, perhaps the unit started the day four tanks short.

The accounts in this chapter confirm six Churchills hit by AP shots, of which three (one on Point 158; two on Point 174) were blamed on anti-tank guns before the Tiger was seen on Point 174; three (Forrest's on Point 144, later finished off by a landmine; Dodson's on Point 158; and Birkbeck's, between Point 170 and Point 174) were attributed to the Tiger after it took position on Point 174. The same Tiger was possibly the killer of a six-pounder gun and its tractor around Point 104.

The 142nd RAC had lost 8 killed and 11 wounded. Birkbeck's second-in-command (Major S.D.G. Robertson) took command at some point: his assumption was written in pencil after the war diary had been typed, which gives Roper all the credit for the withdrawal. Roper had ordered the withdrawal before receiving 2nd Brigade's confirmation, which arrived while the tanks were crossing Point 151.

The 142nd RAC war diary implies that 2nd Brigade HQ was held in low esteem long before. The war diary for the Dukes recorded that their communications with 2nd Brigade had broken down, before the Germans infiltrated into their remaining positions (presumably as far as the crest above the gulley). Their commander (Webb-Carter) passed a message through the Gordons that unless he heard otherwise he would withdraw his battalion at midnight to Point 151. He received no reply, so ordered the withdrawal. By this time, the Dukes were being outflanked. Around then, the commander of the Sherwood Foresters arrived, which was the first time Webb-Carter heard of the relief. Then he heard that 2nd Brigade had cancelled the relief. Nevertheless, the withdrawal to Point 151 was completed. Eventually, the Dukes dug in south of the farm at Kat Zralb for the night, near the Loyals. At 0600 hours, they moved to Snake Ridge, still in reserve, when they started to receive replacements. The Dukes took ten days to reorganize, before they were ready for operations. Even then, they mustered only 13 officers in the fighting echelon (less than half of authorization).

The Loyals had reported 33 officers and 801 other ranks on 1st April; they were now reduced to 14 officers and 520 other ranks. They had lost 15 officers killed or wounded, and 21 killed, 141 wounded, and 82 missing from the other ranks (Dean, 2003, p. 187). Officially, the 2nd Brigade lost 57 killed, 262 wounded, and 190 missing (Playfair, 1966, p. 437). Brigadier Eric Moore remained in command until removal a year later.

CHAPTER 2

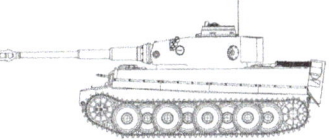

THE SECOND DAY

Tiger 131 had seen off a battalion of Churchill tanks and five battalions of infantry on 23rd April. It would struggle with parts of three battalions of Churchill tanks and six battalions of infantry by the second day, before it succumbed.

Forces

At 0300 hours on 24th April, the 1ID ordered 3rd Brigade to attack the same hills, at dawn. This would be coincident with an attack by 12th Brigade of 4ID towards Peters Corner (the southernmost bend and junction of the Tunis-Medjez highway, 1,400 yards (1,300 m) due south of the right-hand edge of the map). The 10th Brigade was supposed to pass through 12th Brigade, although in the end the assault was not successful enough to permit 10th Brigade.

The depleted Dukes of 2nd Brigade stayed in reserve; the 1st Battalion, King's Shropshire Light Infantry, attacked Point 158, while 2nd Battalion of the Sherwood Foresters attacked Point 174.

They were supported by an improvised battalion of Churchills made up from both tank brigades. The 25TB was in charge, while 21TB's HQ was suffering a still unexplained break-down: at some point in the prior days, Thomas Ivor-Moore's command was suspended, and 48th RTR's Gerry Brooks took over (probably due to refusing orders: see Newsome 2020d). The 25TB was most experienced, but most denuded. The HQ of 142nd RAC commanded three "composite" squadrons: a composite squadron from 142nd RAC of 25TB; a composite Squadron from 145th RAC of 21TB; and the B Squadron from 48th RTR, also of 21TB. Each squadron was reinforced with tanks and crewmen who had passed through their common reinforcement unit. The shortage was of men more than tanks.

The 142nd RAC was a strange choice to command, except that it was experienced in the area since the day before. Contradictorily, its commander had been killed that day (Birkbeck); his deputy (Major Robertson) took over, but barely features in the diary. Major Lyne had commanded its B Squadron on Point 174, but was left out of the final charge that killed Birkbeck, although his composite squadron would be given the lead on 24th April. Perhaps the primacy of 142nd RAC on both days of this battle was driven, at root, by familiarity with 25TB's commander (R.H. Maxwell), who had commanded 142nd RAC until promotion in August.

The 145th RAC had lost at least ten tanks in the hills immediately to the north-west on 23rd April. Nevertheless, it could have rotated in as a complete battalion, rather than submit a composite company under the weaker 142nd RAC.

The 48th RTR was the strongest of the three units, but least experienced. Its only battle to date had been on 21st April, against a Tiger in the pass by Djebel Djaffa, 10 miles (16 km) to the south-west (Newsome 2020d). Within the next two days, its commander (Gerry Brooks) took over 21TB HQ, although his deputy (John Mennel) had been carrying the unit anyway. Its C Squadron was not allocated to battle on 24th April, anymore than on 21st April. The B Squadron was given a supporting role on 21st April and fully committed on 24th April. The A Squadron (which Mennell had formerly commanded) remained at rest on 24th April, although it would be committed on 25th April.

Plans

The improvisations, changes of command, turnover, stresses, and inter-echelon tensions help to explain subsequent confusions over performance. As on the previous day, orders from the brigade echelon and above were unreliable. At 0130 hours, the commander of 145th RAC was summoned to 1ID HQ to receive orders to attack Point 187 – 4,500 yards (4,100 m) directly north of Point 174, with a composite squadron and unit HQ. The 142nd RAC HQ received a warning order at 0300 to support 3rd Brigade from Kat Zralb to Point 174. Both attacks were supposed to start at dawn (0530 hours), but were cancelled at 0500.

The 48th RTR's B Squadron also received a warning order at 0300 hours, via a liaison from 25TB. The order was to assemble at the farmhouse at Kat Zralb. Major Cecil A. "Bill" Joss was called to 3rd Brigade's HQ, but found only the Brigade Major, who was not expecting him and could say only that the Foresters HQ was in the farmhouse.

> The farm was small and somewhat knocked about but in the yard I found a carrier and a staff car and some very sleepy signallers in a slit trench. The occasional mortar came over but otherwise things seemed very quiet. The CO of the 2nd Foresters was asleep in his car and I was sorry to wake him up as his driver told me he had not had any sleep for four days. The CO also was not expecting me and knew nothing of any attack with tanks. He called up his Brigade HQ on the wireless and was told that the brigadier was on his way to see him. When the brigadier [H.A.E. Matthews] arrived, a conference was held at which the CO and the company commanders of the two leading companies attended. The brigadier said he had been ordered

to put in an attack at 0430 hours on Hill 174 with the 2nd Foresters supported by the squadron of tanks I was bringing up. As it was then 0345 and the tanks had not arrived at the M[eeting] P[oint], the ground had not been reconnoitred by me, and there were still two hours of darkness, I was able to persuade the brigadier that the party was not on. I told him I would harbour the squadron somewhere south of the main road, and send a L[iaison] O[fficer] to his HQ to await orders.

At 0300 hours, Joss had ordered his deputy to take the tanks along the highway to its junction with the Grade-3 road (keyed on the map as a road not in good repair) to Kat Zralb, and wait for him there. They left their leaguer at 0325 hours, from just south of Medjez, on the road to Goubellat. The journey measured little more 6 miles (10 km), but, in the dark and with logistical traffic on the highway, they took 90 minutes. Alan Gilmour was driving "Titan."

All that was visible to drivers was the dull glow of exhaust pipes on the tank ahead. Visors had to be open even to see that, letting in icy air and dust which stung the face. The slightest distraction inside the tank was intolerable. Even the red, green, and yellow fascia lights had to be screened. About dawn we were attacked from the air and as the bombs fell hard by, our vehicles bounced on their springs. Throttles wide open, Titan successfully negotiated a ford which was being systematically shelled and bombed, a tense moment.

The bombing slightly damaged Titan's steering and possibly other tanks. Yet the bombing is missing from the war diary and Joss' accounts, which are chronically unreliable. Joss heard the tanks approaching at 0455 hours, so went to meet them (still riding in his staff car). The enemy mortared the junction, for ten minutes, although nobody was hurt. At this point, the crews could get on with their maintenance; Titan's steering brakes were released by disconnecting the compressed air system, leaving fully manual operation of the steering, gears, and clutch. Otherwise, the B Squadron was at full strength in tanks (18 Churchills) and personnel. At 0515 hours, the 16 Churchills from 142nd RAC arrived; eventually, Joss learnt from Lyne that they had the same orders; Lyne clarified that the ultimate objective was Point 174. They decided to harbour just to the south of Snake Ridge, which they completed by 0700.

Unknown to Joss, the commanders of 142nd and 145th RAC were summoned by 1ID to further conferences at 0900. By 0930 hours, the 3rd Brigade's liaison officer took Lyne up to Djebel Hoka (the western end of Banana Ridge: see Map). Djebel Hoka was closer to the units' rest areas, but is lower than the hills to be fought over, so gave no insight to the enemy side, although it might have helped to plan the approaches. Simultaneously, the commanders of 25TB (R.H. Maxwell) and 142nd RAC (Robertson) were reconnoitring somewhere, likely on Snake Ridge, which is higher and closer to the target hills. They were able to trace the track from Point 101 over Point 151 to Point 174. At 1130, Joss received word from his liaison officer (Lieutenant G.H.P. Tyrrell) at 25TB that he should join Maxwell (25TB) and Matthews (3IB) on top of Snake Ridge. Also present were: Robertson and Lyne of 142nd RAC; Major F.J. Reynolds and Major G.G. Bell (respectively the commander and second-in-command of 145th RAC's composite squadron); and the colonel and company commanders from 2nd Foresters. One wonders why such observation was not organized on 22nd April, and why the plan for 24th April varied little from the final charge of 23rd April.

The distinctively camouflaged Churchill IIIs of 145th RAC, hull-down behind a crest, on 6th May, during the final offensive.

According to Joss, the attendees were told that the enemy occupied the entire ridge from Point 174 to Point 158, which would be their objectives. British infantry already occupied Points 144, 151, and 104. They were told also that mines had been cleared along the eastern side of the track from Kat Zralb to Point 151, and from there to Point 144. No intelligence was given about enemy tanks or guns. Then, Robertson and the squadron commanders coordinated their plans for the advance. Joss later reported:

> There was very accurate mortaring going on in the area of the orders group during the whole of the conference. Several fell a bit too close for comfort and it was as if the enemy knew we were there. He was about five miles away so this does not seem likely, but he had not mortared this place. This mortaring did not help me to concentrate, and I went away from the conference with a good knowledge of the plan and method but a poor idea of how the battle was to controlled by Major Robertson and what the wireless layout and code signs were. This was to be our main worry later on.

Joss sent Tyrrell to take the troop commanders up to the same observation post.

> At about 1215 hours the troop officers got back from their recce, complaining a bit that they were mortared all the time they were there and I still had not been able to find out the times of [radio] netting and [was] beginning to get a bit worried. Finally, at 1300, I managed to get a netting call from Major Lyne, who was not the control station but was on net with him. This was unsatisfactory but the best I could do and my out-stations were able to get an indifferent net which they were able to improve slightly later. Wireless communication was, however, extremely bad all day and caused some confusion as will be seen.

At 1230 hours, Lyne radioed his company's officers to gather at the leaguer. He issued orders at 1240 for an attack at 1400 hours. Joss and Lyne had agreed that their squadrons should get ready to leave harbour at 1315, but, due to enemy jamming, the units were forced to organize new radio nets. The 142nd did not reach Kat Zralb until 1410 hours, having travelled 3 miles (5 km) on worn tracks between uncertain minefields, and would need some more minutes to tighten up before starting its advance. The B Squadron of 48th RTR moved at 1335 hours from the same leaguer (south of "Snake Ridge"), after 142nd RAC. However, Joss would write that night to his commander that the attack started on time at 1400 hours, although his later, typed report admitted that his tanks crossed the start line 20 minutes late (i.e., 1420 hours). His war diary appended just ten lines for the day, including the same impossible claim that the attack started on time. The exaggerations and omissions in Joss' letter and thence the war diary will become clearer through this narrative.

Point 158

The composite squadron from 145th RAC had assembled at Kat Zralb around 11 hours earlier, given the short-lived order to attack at dawn. (Its war diary would state that the squadron "returned" to this location after dusk.) Its war diary contains less than three lines on the attack: it describes its objective as "Guerriat Ridge" and "Guerriat el Atach." In fact, it was directed against Point 158, in support of the 1st Battalion of the King's Shropshire Light Infantry. The 145th RAC started on time at 1400 hours, so was never seen by the other tank units. The war diary of the 142nd RAC never mentions 145th RAC, even though the composite squadron from the 145th been assigned (by respective Brigade HQs) under the 142nd's command. This suggests that the 145th acted independently.

The 145th RAC's war diary concluded its mere 2.5 lines on the attack with the claim that "We destroyed a Mk. VI." This is difficult to interpret. The 145th RAC HQ might have meant that its own tanks destroyed the Tiger. However, the vagueness implies an idle boast, after learning that a Tiger had been discovered on Point 174. In any case, no Tiger was destroyed: Tiger 131 was captured intact. At best, the 145th RAC destroyed a dummy.

Point 151

If Tiger 131's abandonment is to be credited to any Churchills, the likelier candidates were on Point 151, which is less than 1,000 yards (900 m) from Point 174, while Point 158 is 1,550 yards (1,400 m) away.

Kat Zralb is 1,200 yards (1,100 m) from the crest of Point 151. The diary of the Sherwood Foresters confirmed that they started on time, because they needed to follow a creeping barrage of smoke and high-explosive shells fired by the divisional artillery and the unit's own mortars.

The Churchill tanks started late and would be curbed by the smoke, dust, radio jamming, landmines, and indirect fire. Joss admitted that by the time he crossed the start line he could already see smoke shells developing on Point 174, and the infantry's mortar carriers deploying on the reverse slope of Point 151. For the infantry, the start line was the track running from north-west to south-east in front of Kat Zralb. Due to landmines, the tanks were not allowed to assemble along it: they formed a column along the track towards Point 151, from south-west to north-east.

Nearer the crest of Point 151, they would need to fan out via the cleared lanes. The leading troops of 142nd RAC left the track too early and lost two tanks on mines. Joss could hear someone shouting over the radio: "Get back on the track at once!" He passed on the same reminder to his own squadron, but urged it forward. Two of his five troops were in front of his tank. Behind him was 7th Troop, in which Gilmour was driving "Titan."

> As we advance, the wireless crackles its demands for speed, "Hurry!" screams the distant voice. "For God's sake, hurry!" We give motors maximum revs, and the big tanks lurch, shudder, and crash over the pitted terrain. We are warned of a minefield in our path. A pause, then frantic voices are on the air as some vehicles strike the hidden mines and blow up. Safely "Titan" negotiates the primrose path. And never ceasing, the din: radio-jamming is producing an insufferable jingle in the headsets, while all the time is the awareness, not as sound but as a physical percussion, a monstrous compression of the air, of shells exploding by us.

After the 142nd RAC lost two Churchills to mines on this side of Point 151, the 48th RTR's leading troop (9th) lost a tank. We know more about the latter thanks to a report by the 48th RTR fitters who recovered it later. It was a Churchill IV that had climbed almost to Point 151 before a German Teller mine smashed two wheels and five track links. The crewmen were repairing the track when a mortar shell landed amongst them, killing the gunner and wounding the driver and commander. The 142nd RAC's squadron was left with 14 tanks; the 48th RTR's B Squadron was left with 17.

None of the war diaries describes respective responsibilities, although Joss' typed report claims that the 142nd RAC was supposed to take hull-down positions on the eastern (right) corner of Point 151, while the 48th RTR took positions on its centre, in order to fire in support of the Foresters. Yet the two squadrons would eventually swap sectors.

By the time Joss reached the cleared lane, the 142nd was still moving about the minefield and trying to reorganize. The first German prisoners were already heading the other way, so he knew that the infantry had advanced ahead without tank support. Joss reported that his two leading troops (9th, 10th) took hull-down positions on the left of Point 151, his HQ to their right, and the following three troops (6th, 7th, 8th) to the right of him. One of 142nd HQ's tanks was nearby, which he presumed to be acting as rear link in the radio net, but he could see no other tanks from the 142nd.

> We were late, but did what we could to support our infantry, who were in the process of winkling out the Germans on 174. This was a dangerous proceeding and of doubtful help to the infantry, and after the CO [of the Foresters] had warned me I ordered the tanks to cease fire.

This panorama was photographed equidistant between the track and Point 151. The track is climbing Gueriat el Atach, north-eastwards. The summit of Point 174 is hidden from Point 151. The map places it 165 yards (150 m) to the right of the track. Photographic distortions make the hill appear to fall away earlier than it really does: the map places the right-most apex of the 170-metre contour about 380 yards (350 m) to the right of the track. Most of the flat of the ridge is hidden from Point 151, which is why the support from Point 151 was useless until the enemy appeared on the horizon. At the same time, although the Germans could dominate Point 174 from the reverse slope, they needed to appear on its crest in order to fire on Point 151. Point 170 is more than 1,650 yards (1,500 m) away, hidden behind the crest, 900 yards (850 m) away. Point 158 is 1,750 yards (1,600 m) away, just left of frame, across a gulley from where the north-western end of Gueriat Ridge falls away.

The 142nd RAC's liaison officer had lost contact with the commander of the Sherwood Foresters, who had continued beyond Point 151. The 142nd blamed the "difficulty of getting tanks on to right flank," which presumably refers to the south-eastern slope of Point 151. None of Joss' documents admits any orders from 142nd RAC, or any deployment to this south-eastern slope, but the 142nd RAC produced the most detailed of the diaries this day:

> During [the] advance, infantry encountered fire from field guns and mortars on the right, and also sighted enemy tanks on the same flank. [The] C.O. [of] Sherwood Foresters asked most insistently for protection on right flank, and eventually a portion of the squadron of 48th RTR was got on position on south-eastern slopes of Pt. 151 at 688364.

The grid reference places this "portion" of B Squadron on the 130-metre contour, facing east and south-east. The "portion" must have been composed of three troops, under Captain Neil R.M. Chadwick. He had been in charge of them from the start, and later would lead them further south-east to Point 144. In 1947, the B Squadron of 48th RTR published a reconstructed war diary:

> The squadron has the task of securing Hill 151 and proceeding to Hill 174. Fierce German resistance is encountered and in addition to the hazards of intense anti-tank fire, uncharted minefields are widespread. The first objective [Hill 151] is secured after sharp skirmishes and exchange of fire.

According to Alan Gilmour: "For two hours, the squadron fights on the hill, which is eventually secured."

Point 174

From the infantry's perspective, the tanks were late and useless. The Sherwood Foresters crossed the crest of Point 151 in extended order: D Company was on the right, B on the left; A and C were 200 yards behind. In the gulley, they ran into landmines and barbed wire, and were enfiladed by machine-guns, mortars, and artillery.

Lieutenant-Colonel R.T.K. Pye went forward, then ordered a barrage from the divisional artillery on the summit of Point 174. The Allies tended to lose the artillery battle in this area over these days. General problems were the inferior calibre and throw-weight of British field guns and the inferior blast and fragmentation of British shells; a local problem was that the Germans held higher observation posts. A particular problem on this day was that the commander of 22nd Field Regiment ("Jock" MacCarthy) was killed on or near Point 174, probably during an attempt to see for himself from the crest: Captain Noel Gee, who brought back his body, was under the impression that he "got himself killed up there on 24th April by taking a wrong turning and driving into No Man's Land," which must refer to the crest.

The infantry cut through the wire, re-started the advance, and got among the enemy's positions. The unit lost four Lieutenants killed that day: the D Company's Lieutenant A. Brachi was attempting to clear a post on his own when he was killed; the fates of the other three were not recorded, so likely the causes were less direct, such as mines and shells. Another two Lieutenants, a Captain, and a Major were wounded, before Pye led the final charge to the summit. Alan Gilmour recalled: "as infantry storm Hill 174, they are met with determined fire from the German guns." In the end, the battalion lost 68 dead (5 officers, 63 other ranks) and 109 wounded – equivalent to about 40 percent of personnel assigned at company echelon. At some point, two companies from the Dukes were placed under Pye's command, presumably after he reported his casualties, after taking the summit (Masters, 1946, p. 8-9).

(Above) This is a dummy Tiger tank, probably in Tunisia or Sicily. Dummy tanks were used extensively by the Germans to tempt Allied bombers, artillery, and tanks away from real threats.

(Below) When viewed from the side, in the shade, through a fuzzy lens, the same dummy is easy to mistake for a real Tiger.

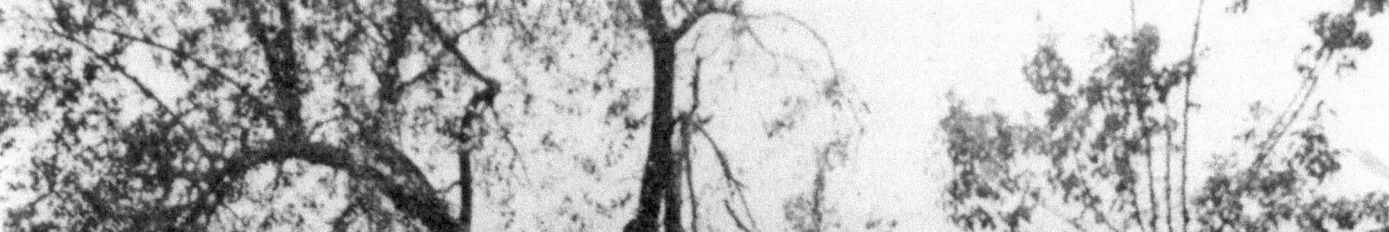

CHAPTER 3

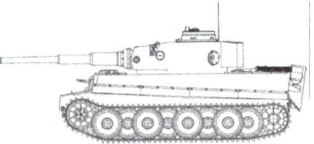

TIGER 131 VERSUS INFANTRY

The ordeal for the Sherwood Foresters did not end with their arrival at the top of Point 174. The hill remained partly in enemy hands, under artillery fire from both sides, and subject to counter-attacks.

Defensive positions

The Foresters did not record their positions. The 142nd RAC recorded that, by the time its liaison caught up around 1600 hours, "the Foresters had occupied the crest of Pt. 174 to the east of the track" and "had great difficulty in holding their positions on the crest." They were being subjected to German counterattacks from the northern and north-eastern slopes (the "forward slopes," from the British perspective). Given these threats, and the experiences of other infantry the day before, the Foresters probably stayed on the reverse slopes and used the crest as cover. The phrase "positions on the crest" could be interpreted to imagine positions on the summit, but tankies tended to use the phrase to refer to the easing gradient between a reverse slope and the flat of the hill, where tanks could take hull-down positions.

The summit would have hidden the British infantry to its south, south-east, and (to a lesser extent) south-west. Likely, the two forward platoons of each of B Company and D Company were near the crest, while the rest of the Foresters were down the reverse slopes. Somewhere, two companies of the Dukes were under the battalion's command – probably in reserve on the other side of Point 151, to where they had withdrawn the day before.

In subsequent days, by when the Foresters had certainly advanced some positions, the official photographs show Foresters still in excavations towards the reverse slope of Point 174, where they would be out of sight to the Germans on the forward slope and the further hills beyond, such as Point 170. German observers on these hills were controlling indirect fire, until those hills were cleared on 6th May.

The German counter-attacks

All the Allied records agree that the Germans counter-attacked on 24th April with infantry and tanks, but are unclear about types and number. The war diary of the 142nd RAC reported that the infantry "were being severely counter-attacked by infantry, supported by tanks." Joss (48th RTR) wrote to his commander: "As soon as objective was held a series of counterattacks were put in with tanks and these provided the main fighting." The ten lines appended to the 48th RTR's war diary changed this to: "Immediately a series of counter-attacks with tanks were put in by the enemy."

The Foresters' war diary recorded: "Objective taken. Consolidation takes place. Counterattacked by Mk. 6 tanks, attack beaten off, position held. Heavy shelling and mortaring caused most casualties."

Tiger 131's counter-attack

The Foresters' entry has been misreported as a counterattack by six Panzers, but the Foresters did not specify the number of Tigers. British tankies on Point 144 would later report five Panzer IVs on the other side of Point 174. The rest of B Squadron, 48th RTR, would claim to knock out a Tiger and at least five other tanks. However, the next day, Lyne would identify six dummy tanks on the other side of Point 174. Dummy Tigers and Panzer IVs would be practically indistinguishable from Point 144.

Only one Tiger was seen on Point 174 itself; and the first Allied photographs of the battlefield (26th April) show only Tiger 131. Perhaps Tiger 131 was the only German tank fighting on Point 174, but was conflated with six dummies. The Allies possibly conflated towed guns too, which the Germans tended to handle more aggressively – by pushing them around in direct support of the infantry, or in the same process of fire and manoeuvre that tanks practiced.

The 142nd RAC's war diary added that "German tanks reached the slopes of Gueriat el Atach [this must mean the reverse slopes, on the British side, as viewed from Point 151] and one tank actually took up a hull-down position on the track at 691373, covering the track back towards 151."

This must have been Tiger 131, repeating the maneuver that had succeeded the previous day. The grid reference places it equidistant between the track and the summit, and on the north-west corner of the 170-metre contour, less than 110 yards (100 m) from the track, about the same distance from the reverse slope, and about the same distance from the summit.

(Upper left) This is one of the three photographs of Tiger 131 in its place of capture (see also page 46). The view is north-eastwards from below the crest, likely on 26th April. (The film was bagged for despatch on the 27th.) The trench (right of frame) was not necessarily ready on the 24th: it might have been dug to take advantage of the Tiger as cover. Indeed, Noel Gee, a FOO, would write that he used Tiger 131 as cover. An official print was given the caption: "The German Mk. 6 Tiger tank in front of our lines, this picture was taken from a trench as the position was under fire from enemy small arms."

(Lower left) A closer photograph, by the same photographer. Tiger 131's shovel was stowed on the front glacis plate, but it is lying on the hull roof, presumably after use by British soldiers. A spade was stowed above the driver.

(Above) The same view photographed in 2019. The road (track) can be seen running left to right behind the tall grass.

(Right) The Pak 97/38 was only 3 feet and 5 inches (1.05 m) tall, so was easy to hide behind the crest. A British official photograph of the rear of such a gun, with three Foresters, was taken on the same day as the photographs at left. It was filed with the caption: "The German anti-tank gun complete with ammo and British crew who knocked out the German Tiger tank." The location is given as "near Medjez-el-Bab." On 11th May, two British newspapers referred to "a German anti-tank gun" that "knocked out" a Tiger. The *Daily Sketch* of Manchester illustrated the claim with one of the photographs of Tiger 131 but no anti-tank gun. The *Press & Journal* of Aberdeen illustrated the claim with the photograph of the gun. The Foresters' war diary records nothing of relevance.

Tiger 131 failed to repel the Foresters. One explanation is prior damage to its turret traverse and gun depression (see the next chapter). Another explanation is topographical. Nobody could see down the reverse slope or over the summit of Point 174 without descending the reverse slope. Even on the level, entrenched infantry are difficult to spot from any tank, and the crew had probably closed hatches due to artillery fire and small arms fire. The Germans were short of infantry as well as tanks, so Tiger 131 was probably acting boldly without direct support. Its crew must have been aware that British infantry were on the hidden side of the crest, but that does not mean the crew could see them.

Tiger 131 versus a PIAT

John Oscroft was in charge of a PIAT in B Company. He was ordered to engage the Tiger. What happened next is not written in any primary source: instead, Oscroft told his son, who publicized the story after his father's death. Thus, we begin his story with speculation rather than quote. We do not know where B Company was positioned. We do not know even what doctrine on use of the PIAT was ever issued to Oscroft. The PIAT had been issued to his division weeks previously, so he had little experience with it, certainly no combat experience.

Naturally, Oscroft would prefer to approach the Tiger's side, and we know that some PIAT gunners, like any anti-tank gunners, were told to avoid the thicker, face-hardened armour on the front of Panzer III and Panzer IV hulls. (They were told to prefer even the front of the turret over the front of the hull.) Whether or not Oscroft himself received this advice, the PIAT projectile's warhead was incapable of piercing Tiger's frontal armour. His story includes his fears of being shot by the turret's machine-gun, but not the hull machine-gun, which suggests that the tank was hull down, or that he never faced its front. Perhaps parts of B Company had already displaced to either side during its approach.

Oscroft crawled forward, presumably from a trench on the reverse side of the crest, as close as he dared. We have no record of what range was trained at the time. The parabolic maximum was beyond 350 yards (320 m). Nominally, the longest of the two ranges allowed by the sights was 100 yards (91 m): the manual described this setting as good for ranges from 85 to 115 yards. Later tests suggest that 75 percent of shots could be fired through a window four-feet square at 100 yards, but while a window is stationary, Tiger 131 was seeking targets. The manual warned that the slow flight necessitates considerable leading of a moving target: "errors in lead and elevation can be corrected by practice and observation of fire, which are always essential." The other aperture in the sights was nominally good for 70 yards (64 m): some official documents suggest that no advantage could be gained by opening fire at closer range, although veterans remembered a consensus that the PIAT was impossible to aim beyond 50 yards (46 m). Certainly, soldiers were encouraged to get close, although the sights were misleading at close range. Later, users were advised that at 20 yards (probably trained as the minimum safe range) they should aim between 2 feet (0.6 m) and 2.5 feet (0.76 m) below the intended impact as viewed through the 70-yard aperture, or aim along the white line painted along the projector.

Range does not affect the effectiveness of the warhead, but Oscroft saw his projectile glance off the turret. Either its impact fuze failed, or the body of the projectile hit before the extended tip (carrying the fuze) could engage. The initial type of fuze was later replaced as unreliable. Without detonation, the projectile is neither hard enough nor energetic enough to leave any evidence of impact (it is propelled by a spring contained within the launcher). If the warhead's shaped-charge (HEAT) had detonated, it would have left a hole less than an inch in diameter, surrounded by tight circles of pitting and spalling. Tiger 131 shows no evidence of any detonation of a shaped charge.

Oscroft said that the turret started to traverse towards him. By then, he was in the open, convinced that the turret machine-gun could kill him. He put his head down, seconds before the turret was hit by an independent projectile.

Tiger 131 versus a towed 75-mm gun

Oscroft was told later that other men from his battalion had fired a captured 75-mm gun. An official photograph proves that this was a PaK 97/38 - a German combination of a 75-mm gun/howitzer (Model 1897) by Schneider of France, with a muzzle brake by Solothurn of Switzerland (to mitigate the recoil of the heavier charge in Polish armour-piercing ammunition), and the carriage of the German 50-mm anti-tank gun (PaK 38). The photograph shows three Foresters posing as if serving the gun. They would have needed to turn the gun around its original German position; they told the official photographer (on 26th April) that the Tiger halted five yards away. However, if the Tiger came that close, Oscroft would have escaped to its side or rear, and could have safely taken a firing position from its side or rear, but neither possibility is part of the story he told his son. Moreover, the photographs do not show tank and gun in the same frame. The photograph shows it with French HE shells, whose fragments cannot explain the damage to the lifting boss or the underside of the armament. Oscroft was aware of only one 75-mm round fired, as Tiger 131 approached. The only evidence in the British photographs for a recent strike on Tiger 131 is a large dark patch in the centre of the driver's plate, perhaps from burnt explosive powder. This was not disabling, but might have contributed to the crew's decision to abandon the tank. Most of the other damage from blast and shell fragments seems to have occurred before Tiger 131's final battle, although their cumulative damage probably contributed to Tiger 131's difficult gunnery on 24th April, as explained in the next chapter.

CHAPTER 4

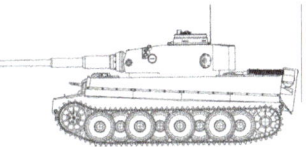

TIGER 131 VERSUS SHELL FIRE

Tiger 131 had been accepted by the 504th Heavy Tank Battalion in February; it reached Tunisia probably in March. It was numbered for 1st Company, 3rd Platoon/Troop, platoon commander. The two German photographs in Tunisia show it damaged by blast and shell fragments before its final battle. Other high-explosive shells damaged Tiger 131 further during its final battle, as proven by the damage that appears in the British but not the German photographs.

External damage

The British infantry fired captured at least one 75-mm high-explosive shell at its front; possibly, the Churchill tanks fired 57-mm and 76-mm shells; and the area was under indirect fire from both sides. The indirect fire continued to fall on the hill after Tiger 131's abandonment, which is the best explanation for the damage to Tiger 131's roadwheels and skirts on its left side, and to the fittings on the rears of the turret and hull (given that a centrifugal air cleaner on the left rear is visible in one of the German photographs and is in good condition).

Shell strikes are difficult to count because they produce fragments, rather than a single impact per projectile. The damage seen in the German photographs can be summarized in five main areas (not necessarily from as many shells):
1. the commander's cupola, facing front;
2. the upper front of the turret;
3. the turret mantlet, particularly to the left (nearside) of the main armament;[1]
4. the base of the main armament, particularly to its left; and
5. the upper edge of the driver's plate (again, to the left of the main armament).

The British photographs show additional damage from fragments in seven areas, which probably occurred during and after Tiger 131's final battle, given that an undamaged air cleaner is visible in one of the German photographs:
1. the centrifugal air cleaners (by Eugen Feifel), either side of the exhausts;
2. the shields around the two exhausts;
3. the cowlings or grills above the engine compartment;
4. the rear of the stowage bin on the back of the turret;[2]
5. the side skirts towards the rear;
6. the roadwheels, particularly on the left side; and
7. the loader's hatch.

Turret traverse

The photographs do not reveal the internal damage. No German records for Tiger 131 have survived; and British observations of the damage are surprisingly unsystematic. Yet the internal damage was significant enough to affect Tiger 131's lethality. Probably the most alarming damage, from the crew's perspective, was to the turret traverse.

The turret traverse suffered damage at several positions, separate to the damage of the turret ring at the 12 o'clock position due to a ricochet off the underside of the main armament during its final battle (described later). The high-explosive blasts probably acted through the turret to warp the turret ring or damage the turret race. Trials in Britain found that the traverse was most difficult rightwards (clockwise) from the 9 o'clock position, where the necessary force was so great that the handwheel clutch slipped.[3] Thus, in the event of a drop in hydraulic pressure, such as if the engine were to stall, the gunner could traverse leftwards only from this position.

---

1. Sometimes visitors ask about the apparent dents at each side edge of the mantlet. Each edge has two depressions, overlapping each other, one above the other. These depressions are pinch marks left behind during the casting of the mantlet.
2. The stowage bin was never repaired or replaced: a captured stowage list prescribes stowage of a tarpaulin, 10 track links, and 10 track pins; no record has survived of the contents of Tiger 131's stowage bin.
3. The Gunnery School's Experimental Wing received Tiger 131 in March 1944. Its report notes: "There is a foul caused by damage between 9 and 10 o'clock when the loads rose to 60 pounds [27.2 kg] right and 45 pounds [20.4 kg] left, and the turret jammed. At this point it could not be rotated owing to the clutch slipping." The clutch slipped when the traverse was being effected via the handwheel; presumably, the hydraulic system could overcome the friction, although the report does not clarify. In any case, the crew probably maintained a bias to leftwards traverse by either manual or hydraulic power. The next highest load was recorded when turning right from each of the 5 and 7 o'clock positions. Traverse from other positions could be as light as ½ pound (0.2 kg). The leftwards traverse was stickiest between 12 o'clock (16 pounds; 7.3 kg) and 11 o'clock (17 pounds; 7.7 kg). See: Newsome, 2020b.

(Above) This is the earliest British photograph to focus on the mantlet, circa mid-May 1943. The German photograph of Tiger 131 (see page 11) proves that most of the damage occurred before the battle for Gueriat el Atach, from shells bursting above or on the upper mantlet. The pitted appearance around the bulge of the mantlet is an artifact of the sand mould; the pits would help fragments to bite. Even the apertures for the gunsight are nicked. An AP shot scooped the left lifting boss, sometime after the German photograph, probably on 24th April. Another shot skimmed the underneath of the gun and cracked the hull roof at the 12 o'clock position, which is right of frame (the gun is currently at 2 o'clock).

(Left) These fragments of HE shells were collected from Point 174 in 2019. They are of sufficient size and weight to cause scars like those on Tiger 131.

(Right) The tops of Tiger 131's main armament and mantlet show irregular scoring from fragments of shells bursting above and to the left of the gun. The number "40," on the centre top of the mantlet, was welded by the Germans.

The turret was easier to traverse leftwards than rightwards from most positions. Even if the traverse had not been damaged, the return to the 12 o'clock position from the 9 o'clock position would take three times longer going leftwards (counter-clockwise) than rightwards (clockwise). On Tiger 131, counter-clockwise traverse was increasingly difficult from about the 3 o'clock position to a peak between the 12 and 11 o'clock positions – where the traverse required 34 times more force than the easiest position.

Gun elevation and depression

The high-explosive impacts on the mantlet are the best explanations for damage to the gun's counter-balance. In early models of Tigers, including Tiger 131, the counter-balance consisted of mechanical linkages, anchored inside the upper right corner of the mantlet, and acting on a hydraulic cylinder. (In the new turret design, from the 820th Tiger, in January 1944, the counter-balance was relocated to the rear, behind the commander's seat, connected to the mantlet via pulleys and a chain, which would not transmit shocks from the mantlet.) The damage resulted in inconsistent friction and springing at different angles of elevation. Colonel Willie Blagden was the first to report on Tiger 131: he was the highest technical authority at the British Army's Middle East Command in Cairo; he arrived in Tunisia in May, with several investigative tasks, including a review of Tigers. After operating Tiger 131, around 14th May, he reported that "[t]he gun appears stiff to elevate but depresses quite easily." This was confirmed by the British Gunnery School's trials in April 1944: control was unreliable, such that the gun's elevation was thrown off every time the gun fired – by 16 to 19 minutes. This damage was rediscovered during the Tank Museum's restoration of the tank in 1999 (the first time the tank had been disassembled since 1944). For some reason, the first disassembly (around Summer to Fall 1944) was not documented. At some point, Tiger 131 was reassembled (probably in 1945), again without documentation.

Internal fittings

The vibration of the turret from blast could explain the loss of the most delicate internal fittings. After inspecting Tiger 131 on 14th May, Blagden reported that the eyepieces for the gunner's binocular-telescopic sights were missing. They were never found. They would be replaced in Britain with eyepieces recovered from a different Tiger.

Moreover, the clinometer beside the telescopic sights was missing its electrical wiring and bulb for illumination. Possibly these items were ripped out by souvenir hunters, but these would be innocuous parts to steal. The Germans probably did not salvage anything – they left the machine-guns, which were normally the first items for salvage. Most likely, the parts were dislodged by external attack, then lost when the interior was cleaned.

Versus machine-guns

Unfortunately, an alternative theory needs to be refuted at this point. In the 2000s, the Tank Museum asked a sometime-lecturer in crime forensics from a local university to interpret the damage.[4] He concluded that Tiger 131 was struck on both sides and the front by machine-gun fire. He claimed that one burst hit the hull's left towards the rear, at an angle of about 10 degrees; and another burst hit the hull's right and most of the road wheels, from an angle of about 30 degrees. Counting a burst on the front of the mantlet, he got to a total of 30 bullets (Fletcher et al, 2011, p. 37).

Thirty would be an unusually small number for a tank supposedly machine-gunned on three sides, but that's only one theoretical problem. The copper jacket and lead core of "ball" ammunition could not cause the large and deep scarring of Tiger 131's armour. Ball ammunition relies on inertia to perforate harder materials (termed "overmatching" at the time and since): it can overmatch armour plates only a few millimetres thick. It would leave no evidence on thicker plates except brown and grey residues. The first photographs of Tiger 131 show no evidence for such residues. Any residues would have been removed since by cleaning, re-painting, shot-blasting, and more re-painting. The anti-magnetic application known as *Zimmerit* would have been chipped by bullets, but was not standardized by the Germans until September 1943.

AP bullets are hard enough to leave an impression in armour,[5] but the British issued no AP bullets to their tanks or infantry, due to inferior accuracy, greater wear on the barrel, and greater burden of manufacture.

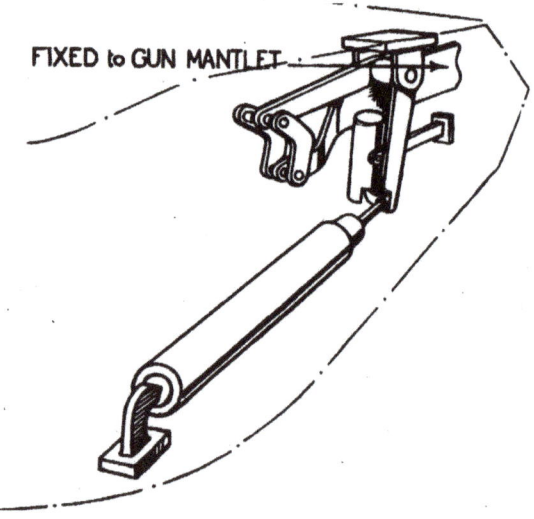

This drawing of Tiger 131's counter-balance appeared in STT's report of February 1944.

4. David Schofield no longer works for Bournemouth University and could not be reached for comment. At the time, he worked for the university's School of Conservation Sciences, and directed a programme in safety management; previously he worked as a public health inspector. See: Moore and Lakha, 2007.

The sometime-lecturer in crime forensics reported all bullet strikes as 7.7-mm (0.303-inch), but only the infantry fired 7.7-mm bullets; Churchill tanks mounted 7.92-mm (0.312-inch) machine-guns. Possibly, the crews of the Churchills at Gueriat el Atach were using captured German armour-piercing rounds (also of 7.92 mm calibre), which had been recommended in 1941 by technicians in Egypt for firing through the shields of enemy artillery guns. However, higher authorities discouraged such use as dangerous and inefficient. None of the Churchill crews or units left any evidence of any use of armour-piercing bullets. As relatively inexperienced crews, they were least likely to try.

Even armour-piercing bullets would not explain the largest and most irregular impacts. Likely, the damage seen on Tiger 131 was caused by large calibre high-explosive shell fragments before 24th April, except for one 75-mm HE shell strike on the driver's plate on 24th April, and two 57-mm AP shots (one to the left-hand lifting boss; and one underneath the main armament, as explained in the following chapters).

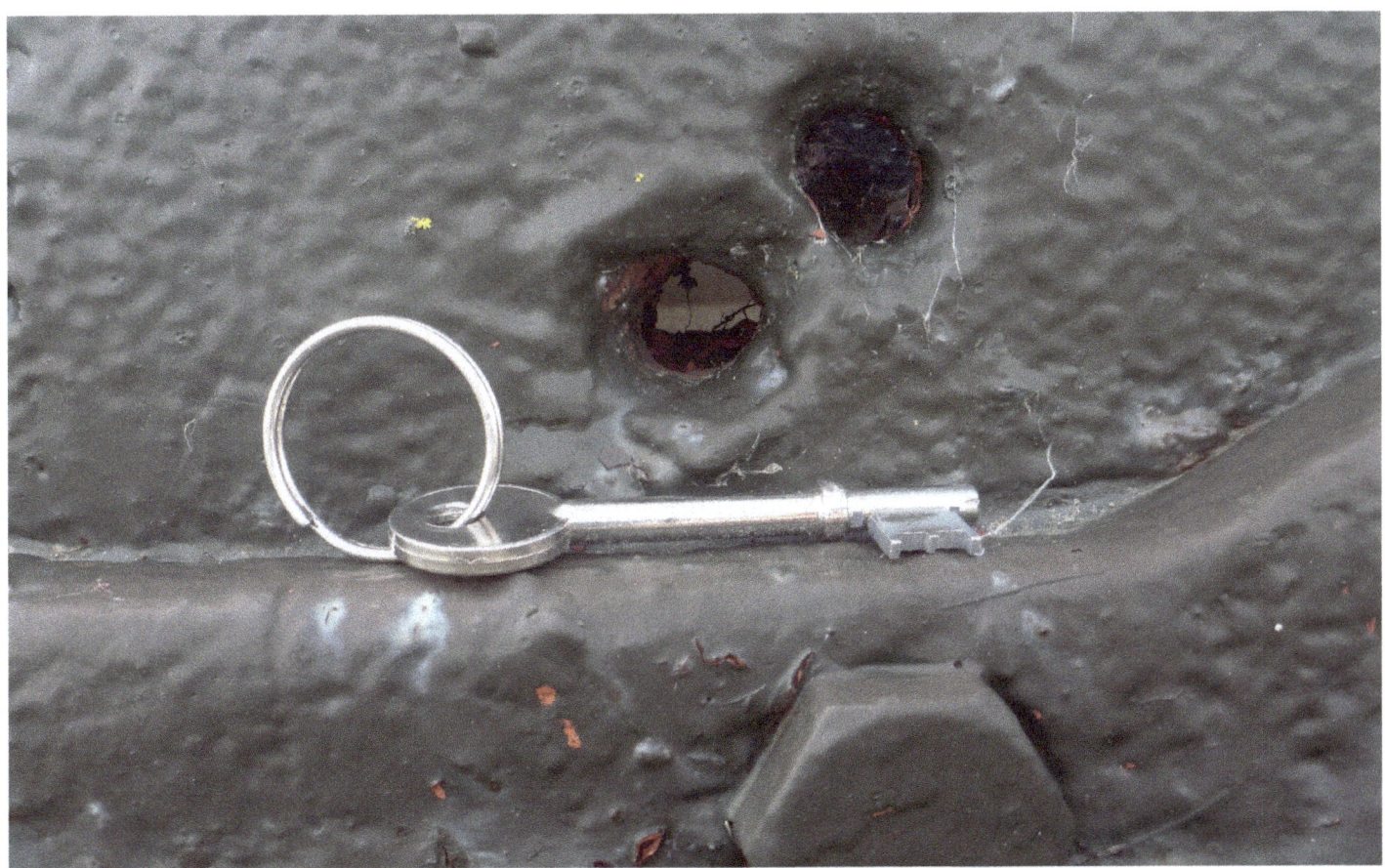

(Above) These neat holes were made by two 7.62-mm or 7.92-mm AP bullets, through 20-mm of rolled homogenous armour, to British IT70 specification, which was softer than Tiger's armour (Newsome 2020f). The plate formed the front of a turret taken from a Cruiser V (Covenanter) and placed as a target on a British range. None of the damage to Tiger 131 is so neat.

(Overleaf, upper left) The backside of Tiger 131's driver's plate is pitted by fragments travelling from the rear. The horizontal roof plate collects rainwater where it is still bowed from the downward impact of the 57-mm shot in 1943.

(Overleaf, lower left) The driver's plate is scored on both sides, particularly the rear face. This damage was not caused by a shot, which would have perforated from one side to the other.

(Overlead, upper right) The bottom and top edges of the skirt at the left rear were perforated by fragments.

Overleaf, lower right) The centrifugal air cleaners towards the right of the rear plate show damage from fragments travelling from the right front. The dents are from blast or collisions. (On top of one of the cleaners is a collection of foreign objects recovered from Tiger 131's engine compartment during overhaul at the Tank Museum in 2018.)

5. British 7.7-mm steel-cored APCR projectiles could penetrate 11.3 mm of British rolled armour, at best (T.P. (Armour), Ministry of Supply, "Armour for Fighting Vehicles," June 1941). German 7.92-mm projectiles could penetrate from 8.8-mm (steel-cored APCR-T) to 19 mm (tungsten-carbide-cored APCR) (War Office, MI10, Technical Intelligence Summary Number 54, 20th September 1941).

(Above) This panorama of photographs was taken just below Point 174, on its western side: Montarnaud is more than 3,000 yards (2,800 m) away from the camera. The track heads north-eastwards, before a left turn to Montarnaud. The outer edges of this panorama curve around to the north (left) and east (right). Point 170 is due north, less than 1,000 yards (900 m) away, but is hidden by an intervening crest, 510 yards (470 m) away.

(Below) This panorama of photographs was taken at an elevation of about 172 m, on the south-western slope or reverse slope, on the Allied side of Point 174. The summit is to the left and rear of the camera. Tiger 131 did not advance this far: it did not need to expose itself on this downslope: it maintained a somewhat hull-down position on the other side of the crest, behind the camera, although it had advanced up the forward slope in order to get line of sight on Point 144, Point 151, and points north.

Point 144 is less than 1,500 yards (1,350 m) away, due south. Point 151 is 900 yards (830 m) away, to the south-west. Kat Zralb is less than 2,000 yards (1,800 m) away. Point 104 is more than 1,700 yards (1,550 m) away, due west. Point 158 is less than 1,600 yards (1,460 m) away, but is hidden behind the rest of Gueriat el Atach, which does not fall away significantly until 900 yards (820 m) from the camera.

CHAPTER 5

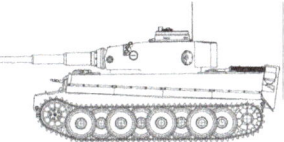

TIGER 131 VERSUS CHURCHILL TANKS

While confronting the infantry, Tiger 131 was exposed to fire from the Churchill tanks, up to its abandonment.

Point 151

As shown in Chapter 2, Major S.D.G. Robertson (142nd RAC's acting CO) had sent part of B Squadron, 48th RTR, to the south-eastern corner of Hill 151. This part likely consisted of three troops, under Captain Neil R.M. Chadwick (a total of 10 tanks). The grid reference places this part of B Squadron on the 130-metre contour, facing east and south-east. Nobody recorded the timing, but the move cannot have occurred before 1500 hours. After 1600 hours, the 142nd RAC's liaison officer re-connected with the commander of the Sherwood Foresters. As the war diary tells the story, this was around the time when Tiger 131 re-took its commanding hull-down position between the track and the summit of Point 174. Robertson decided not to advance any tanks towards Point 174, but to send Chadwick's group to Point 144.

> Sherwood Foresters had great difficulty in holding their positions on the crest, and the C.O. demanded immediate assistance by our tanks. The message reached Major Robertson in time to get a force of approx. nine tanks over to the right flank.

Point 144

The commander of B Squadron (Joss) does not mention any maneuvers in his letter to his commander, but his later typed report claims that he sent three troops (6th, 7th, 8th) with Captain Chadwick to Point 144, on his own initiative. Joss stayed behind the crest of Point 151 with his tank, another HQ tank (Captain Maurice Rand), and two troops (a total of seven tanks, assuming only one loss for the squadron so far this day: 9th Troop's loss coming up to Point 151). Joss ordered his gunner to fire two 76-mm smoke shells to obscure Chadwick's tanks. All arrived safely, despite crossing part of the uncleared minefield.

The Gordon Highlanders were still occupying Point 144 with two companies forward, and two on the hill behind. They had an easier time this day, receiving less indirect fire and no counter-attacks. Point 144 is 1,000 yards (900 m) south-east of Point 151, and 1,600 yards (1,500 m) south of Point 174, with direct line of sight towards both summits and everything in between. Joss was under the impression, by the time of his report, that Chadwick "dominated a large open area sloping down from 174 to Montarnaud." In fact, the ridge from Point 174 continues south-eastwards, at a range of about 1,400 yards (1,300 m) from Point 144: thus, this shoulder of the ridge obscures Montarnaud, and the 2,200 yards (2,000 m) of reverse slope towards Montarnaud. Moreover, the slopes were covered by mature wheat, in which the British tankies struggled to find the enemy's positions.

On the extreme right, the 8th Troop kept moving up and down, trying to observe Point 174 without loitering. The radio net was still subject to jamming, so Chadwick was forced to co-ordinate everything by running between tanks. Chadwick's tank was least useful anyway, being armed with a two-pounder in the turret.

Within 8th Troop, Corporal Norville reported that he could differentiate enemy from friendly infantry on Point 174, although Lieutenant Palmer decided that they should not fire. Then an 88-mm shot passed through the left-side louvre and the upper track of Norville's tank. He ordered his driver to reverse, before he realized that the track was broken. Unwilling to repair the track under mortar fire, he ordered the crew into a trench. (Due to the same mortar fire, this tank would not be recovered for days.) Norville had not seen the shooter.

Palmer changed position to orient towards the right without exposing himself to Point 174, but he was mistaken: a shot carried away the eighth roadwheel on his left side and exploded under the belly plate below the engine. Palmer noticed smoke, but since the engine temperature gauge remained normal he assumed no trouble, and continued to manoeuvre out of trouble. (In fact, the cooling system had been damaged, so this tank too would fall out of action soon.) Then a shot perforated the side turret plate of a tank in 6th Troop, killing the loader.

These side shots must have come from Tiger 131. Joss blamed "88-mm guns from the area of Montarnaud and Pt. 174. These were extremely difficult to locate as they were firing at 2,000 yards." However, Montarnaud did not have line of sight on Point 144, and is more than 4,200 yards (3,900 m) away. Joss never visited Point 144, not even after the battle. More likely, the shooter was behind Point 174, about 1,500 yards (1,350 m) away.

Tiger 131's demise

Major Joss remained on Point 151 throughout the many diversions and attacks, so should be the best source for events on Point 151, but his letter to his commander exaggerated his successes and did not explain his losses. That letter contained no claim to knock out a Tiger directly. Later, in his typed report, Joss added a claim that he must have heard later from Captain RAND: Joss wrote that his nearest troops knocked out a Tiger in motion on Point 174, just after the Tiger had set alight a Churchill of 142nd RAC on the left (north) side of the track between Kat Zralb and Point 151. He estimated the range as 1,000 yards (914 m). Indeed, the summits are exactly this distance apart.

> [Point 174] was now occupied by our troops and there was no sign of the enemy. There was a little mortaring but we kept changing our positions and managed to avoid trouble. Then over the wireless came the information that the enemy were putting in a counter-attack on 174, with tanks, and we were to keep a look-out for these. Shortly afterwards, Captain Rand saw an aerial mast moving along the ridge of 174. He put his gun on to it and informed the rest of 9th Troop. The tracks appeared and the tank was identified as a Mark VI. As we had to be absolutely sure that this was a German tank, he told his Troop to hold their fire until the whole of the turret was visible, but one of 10th Troop opened fire so Captain Rand gave the order to open fire also. [Rand himself probably did not fire, because his tank was likely a close-support variant, armed with a two-pounder and a 76-mm howitzer.] He was rather nervous of opening fire as there was one of our infantry carriers just below the Mark VI and at 1,000 yards he thought an under [a projectile falling short of target] might hit the carrier. This unfortunately happened [this carrier might have been in use by the CO of the Foresters for scouting: see page 47] but the Mark VI disappeared and came up again in a different position and was hit. The crew bailed out and were shot by our infantry.

Two AP shots certainly hit Tiger 131 (one carried away the left lifting boss; the other skimmed the underside of the main armament). Both are consistent in size with shots fired from 57-mm six-pounder guns, which armed most of the Churchills there. The infantry had no towed six-pounders yet, only 40-mm two-pounders and the captured 75-mm Pak 97/38. The likeliest shooters were Churchills around Point 151, which included not just B Squadron of the 48th RTR but also part of the composite squadron and the HQ of 142nd RAC. Some Churchill tanks were in the gulley or on the reverse slope of Point 174, but could not see the Tiger behind the crest.

The likeliest date of impact is 24th April. Several tanks of the 142nd RAC had claimed to strike a Tiger the previous day, but then we would expect the jammed turret to have been repaired before Tiger 131 was committed on the 24th.

The lifting boss

The easiest of the two shots to describe is the non-disabling shot, although this was not necessarily the first hit. A shot scooped the mild steel lifting boss welded to the turret's left side (nearside). The hull shows no evidence that the shot glanced off the tank first.

The shot travelled at an unusual upward angle of more than positive 30 degrees. The difference in elevation from Point 151 to Point 174 is insufficient to explain this upward angle, so the shot must have deflected off the crest or the carrier just in front of the Tiger. Even if we imagine a Churchill tank coming around the south-eastern corner of Point 151, fully exposed to Tiger 131, at a range of 950 yards (870 m), the difference in elevation between the summit is only 23 metres or 1.6 degrees (2.8%). Even if we imagine the firer on the steepest uptick of the reverse slope, as close as 440 yards (400 m) from the summit, and Tiger 131 on the summit, the angle barely rises above 4 degrees (7.5%). A shot can change direction after impact, but the scoop is smooth and linear.

Under the armament

A separate shot skimmed the underside of the 88-mm barrel. The first British photographs of the tank show that the main armament is slightly depressed – consistent with a hull-down position while aiming down to a lower elevation. However, the gun would have fallen as hydraulic pressure declined after abandonment.

The shot first scooped the gun above the driver's plate, without striking the driver's plate or anywhere else on the hull. The hull of the tank is undamaged forward of the shot's first impact.

The shot's travel has a rightwards, downwards bias after first impact, consistent with the clockwise (right-handed) spin of any shot fired through the right-handed rifling of most firearms, including the French 75-mm and the British 57-mm. The travel and the scorings are inconsistent with a fragment from a shell. The shot engaged the underside of the sleeve three times; then it struck, in rapid succession, the bottom edge of the flared base, the bottom edge of the bolted anchor, and thence the bottom edge of the mantlet; from there, it was deflected slightly downwards, so that it struck the horizontal roof plate, before sliding into the bottom edge of the turret ring. The shot struck when the gun was slightly right (offside) of the centre line, as proven by the damage to the central joint of the hull roof.

The flight was almost horizontal, along the underside of a depressed gun, so its angle of attack on the hull roof was too slight to perforate directly. It buckled the horizontal plate just to the left (nearside) of the central joint, and ended up digging into the turret ring. The damage to the hull roof is slightly closer to the driver (on the left or nearside) than the radio operator (on the right or offside). The shot might have fragmented during any of its strikes. Some of these fragments might have perforated the joint, but we have no confirmation of fragments inside the tank. The best source is the man who eventually recovered Tiger 131: Major Douglas Lidderdale commanded the 104th Army Tank Workshops, which served the two brigades of Churchill tanks in Tunisia. He first visited Tiger 131 on 6th May; he kept notes that he

(Below right) This view gives the clearest evidence that a single shot caused the scoring along the underside of the barrel, mantlet, and turret ring. Note that no shot has damaged the proud upper edge of the driver's plate, or the proud cover for the air intake vent in the roof between the hull machine-gunner and driver. The shot's first strike was on the underside of the gun, nearest the camera. The gun is elevated for this photograph, but would have been depressed at the time of strike.

(Below left) This close-up is of the scoop taken out of the turret's lefthand lifting boss. The projectile escaped rearwards and upwards, probably without striking again. The smoke discharger on this side had been damaged earlier, as shown in the German photograph.

soon turned into a report, although it would not be officially published until shortly after he arrived with Tiger 131 at the School of Tank Technology, in Britain, in November. This report contains the following description:

> The general condition of the vehicle is reasonably good both structurally and mechanically.
>
> Heavy frontal attack is in evidence at the front of the vehicle. An oblique hit which registered at 12 o'clock on the superstructure top plate [roof] has fractured the lateral weld along the centre of the plate. The round struck the turret ring joint damaging the pneumatic sealing tube and jamming the turret traverse. The blow on the top front plate also resulted in the complete disintegration of the wireless set.
>
> There are no penetrations of the armour although the vehicle has been subjected to heavy fire, the front vertical plate [driver's plate] and the turret front being considerably scarred. Apart from a minor defect in the starting apparatus the vehicle was in good mechanical condition when received in this country.

Note that Lidderdale clarifies explicitly that no round penetrated any plate – the left-hand hull roof was dented, the joint with the right-hand horizontal plate was cracked, the turret ring was damaged, but the round did not perforate.

Lidderdale reported that the radio was smashed by the time he arrived, which he attributed to the impact on the roof, although German crews conventionally removed or disabled radios before evacuation. The first photographs prove that his men removed the damaged radio during the few days before official photographers reached his workshops. Both Lidderdale and Blagden recorded in May that the speedometer and engine revolutions counter were broken (and remained broken in England), but the photographs show no damage to their faces, suggesting that the external shock broke their internal mechanism without any ingress of fragments.

This photograph focuses on the impact to the base of the gun sleeve, the mantlet, and the turret ring. The welded seam in the hull roof plate is obvious. The filled scoop/dent is mostly hidden by the handle for the axe (not original to the vehicle).

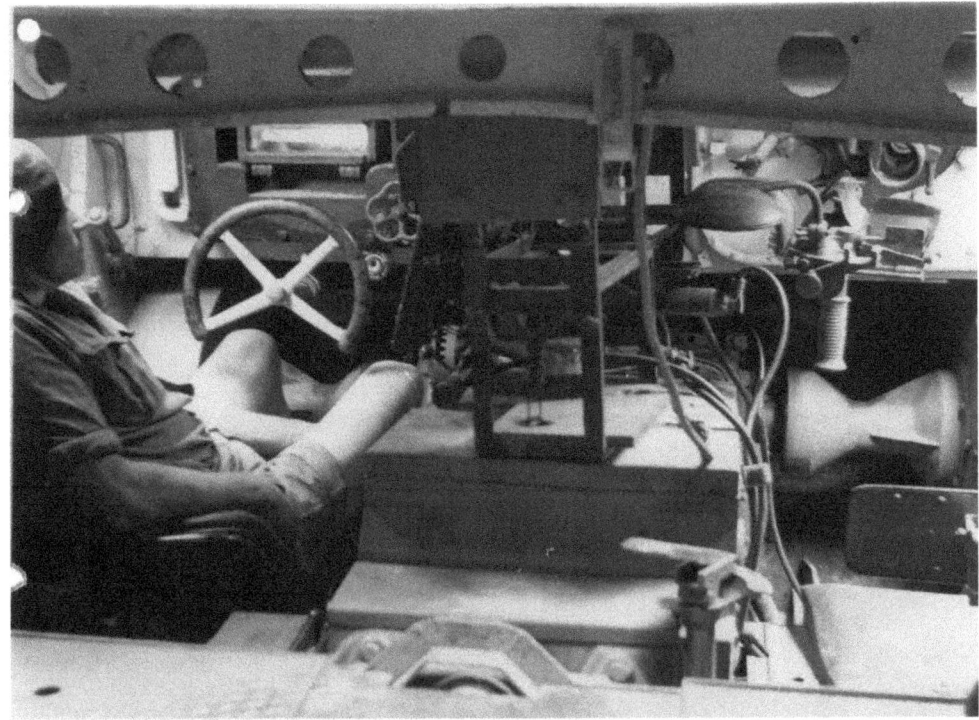

This photograph was taken from the floor of the fighting compartment, looking forward towards the driver's position (left) and machine-gunner's position (right). Between them, the brackets in the centre should carry the radios, but the radios have been removed by now. The photograph was probably taken just after the campaign in Tunisia ended on 13th May, when units had the opportunity to catch up with orders to switch to "tropical" clothing. Tiger 131 was recovered on 7th May.

At some point, presumably in May, the damage to Tiger 131's hull roof plate was repaired by Lidderdale's team with welds and a D-shaped metal plug. No record survives of this repair. No photographs of the area before the repair were taken. The best appreciation can be derived from this oblique photograph of the area after shot blasting in December 1991.

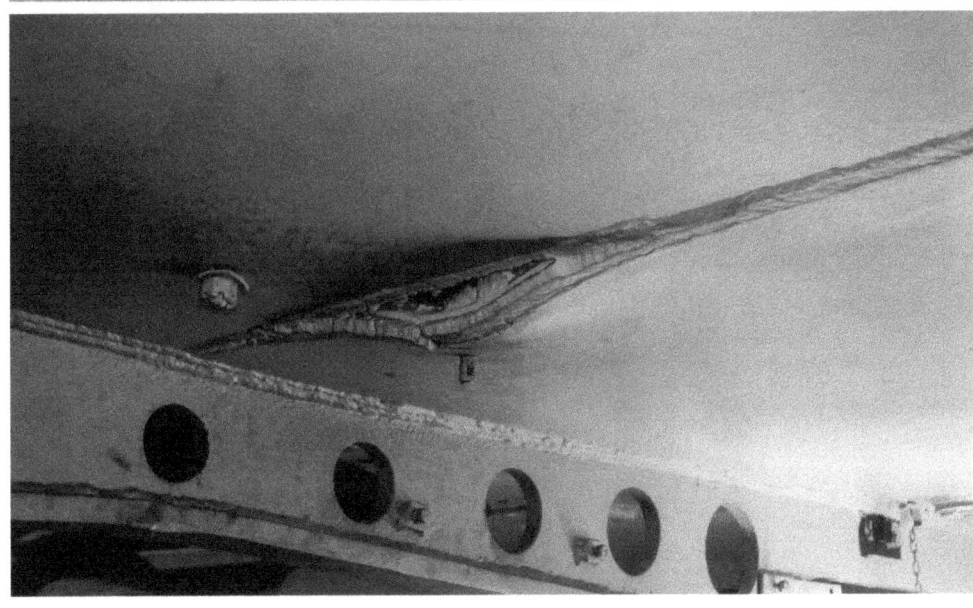

This photograph was taken during the same period of restoration, circa December 1991. The photographer is sitting in the hull machine-gunner's position, looking leftwards and rearwards towards the centre-line. The scoop and dent were never righted. Instead, the depression was simply filled with metal, roughly flush with the rest of the roof.

No evidence of casualties was found inside Tiger 131. Joss' typed report contained the hearsay that the "crew bailed out and were shot by our infantry," although Lidderdale later wrote that the "Tiger's radio was shattered by the round which split the weld on the top plate, [and] it is presumed to have incapacitated the driver and the front gunner." The opening of the left-hand side of the overhead joint, and the greater damage to the radio than the instrument panel, suggests that the radio-operator would be most affected. On the other hand, in 1991 the restorers of Tiger 131 realized that the driver's hatch and driver's steering wheel are not original to the tank, although they may have been damaged after evacuation. Even if the two men were uninjured, the shot would have been shocking. Although the tank remained drive-able, the driver might have assumed differently, given the apparent damage to his right and above.

Damage to the turret traverse

Lidderdale wrote that the shot "struck the turret ring joint damaging the pneumatic sealing tube and jamming the turret traverse," which suggests that the sealing tube itself jammed to turret. However, the tube is brass, which is softer and more elastic than steel. Possibly the impact pushed the turret ring against the turret race, or fragments from the shot jammed the space between the bottom of the turret wall and the hull roof plate. Whatever happened, he soon repaired it. He did not record how: no photographs show any removal of the turret in Tunisia, so probably he ground away the fouling on the exterior of the turret ring, and forced the traverse to wear down any burr on the turret race. Lidderdale probably did not need to traverse the turret except to allow access to the engine compartment, given that all his operational demonstrations were automotive. Photographs show that he traversed rightwards to 3 o'clock, so that the engine decks could be opened, and leftwards to 11 o'clock, to demonstrate a hull-down profile. Probably he had discovered that the traverse was more difficult leftwards, given damage suffered by Tiger 131 before Gueriat el Atach.

Loader's hatch

Only two strikes can be attributed to AP shots. The earliest British photographs show perforations of the loader's hatch, but these were probably caused by fragments from shells, after a crewman had left it open during escape. The lecturer in crime forensics suggested that the damage was caused by a single 57-mm shot (Fletcher et al, 2011, p. 36), but the perforations are too numerous, large, and ragged to be caused by a single shot. The original hatch does not survive: Lidderdale's team replaced it, before enshipment to Britain.

This sectional drawing of Tiger 131's turret ring and race was produced at STT, around December 1943, and first published in STT's report on Tiger 131's fighting arrangements, in February 1944.

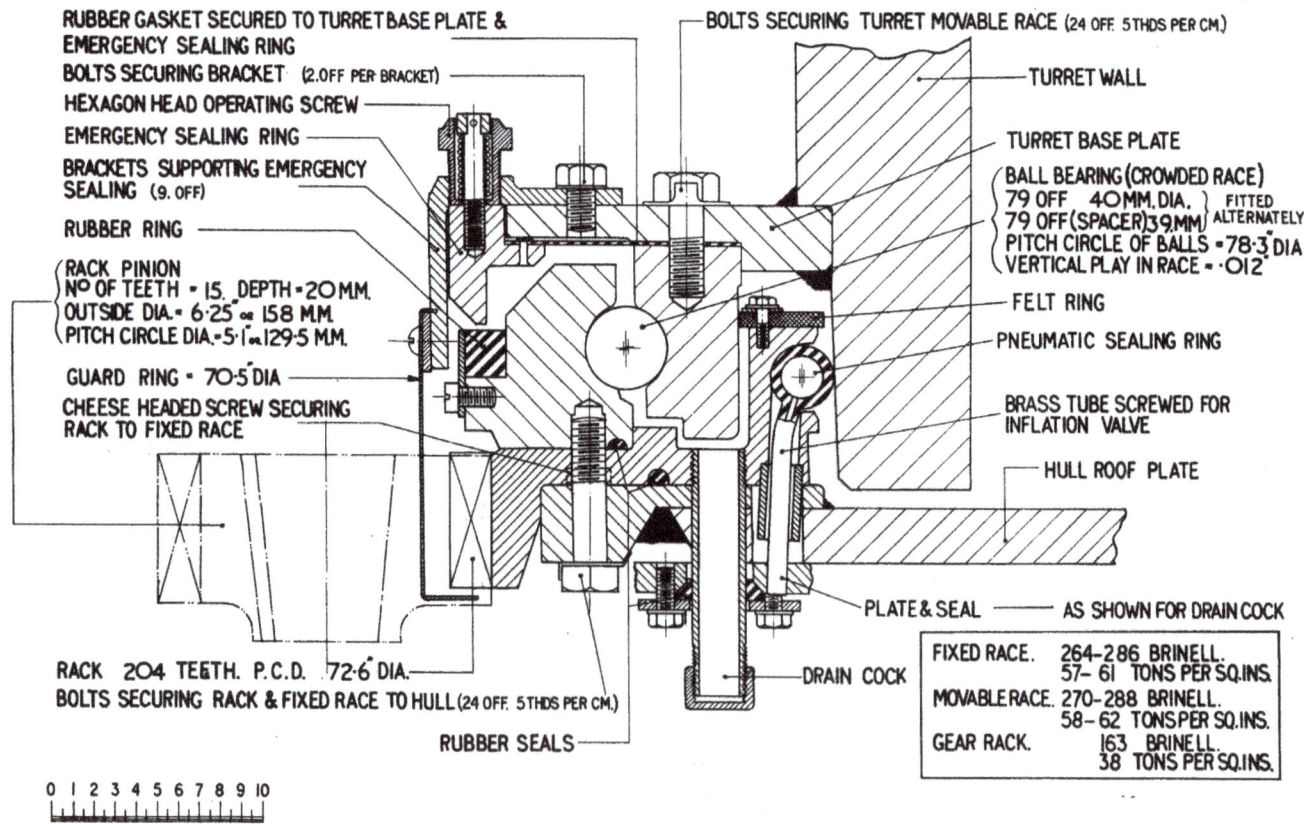

(Above) Brigadier Cooke (1st Army's BRAC, wearing the Royal Rank Regiment's black beret) points out the commander's position to King George VI and Lieutenant-General Kenneth Anderson (1st Army's commander) on 18th June 1943 in Tunis.

(Left) The same damage can be seen today, from large fragments of a shell bursting on or above the turret's front. The German photograph (see page 11) proves that these marks were received before 24th April.

Commander's cupola

Peter Gudgin, who falsely claimed that Tiger 131 was knocked out during his battle at Djebel Djaffa on 21st April (Newsome 2020d), also claimed a six-pounder hit "on the gun mantlet, which could have wounded the commander" (1996, p. 92). The Tank Museum repeated his claim (Fletcher, 1986, p. 56).[6]

However, Gudgin never specified any argument or evidence. In fact, the cupola shows no more damage today than apparent in the German photograph taken before the battle. The Churchills probably deployed no 57-mm shells yet, and had no reason to fire them at a Tiger.

6. When asked in 2019, 23 years later, David Fletcher, the Tank Museum's Historian, reasonably could not remember who had led him to this error, except that the Tank Museum was treating Gudgin as the primary authority on Tiger 131 at the time.

(Above) Fragments damaged the stowage bin, but not the engine compartment or engine, so likely came from a burst to the rear, rather than overhead.

(Left) Lidderdale's team replaced the damaged loader's hatch in Tunisia. This view is from its left rear, showing damage to the rim. This view shows also two scoops or holes, roughly filled with welds. They do not feature in any British records. The two welds shown are in a line of three. Another two are closer to the mantlet. Each measures about 3 inches (76 mm). Their conformity suggests they were bored by the British to test the armour. Perhaps they chose this plate as exemplary of the armour as a whole, without being as visible as the thicker plates.

CHAPTER 6

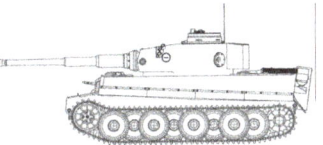

CHURCHILLS ON POINT 174

Upon Tiger 131's abandonment, the Churchills tried to get on Point 174, but would suffer more casualties than ever.

From Point 144

At around 1700 hours, Robertson ordered Chadwick's group to take hull-down positions on Point 174. Chadwick was probably not intimidated: his squadron commander and acting unit commander later agreed that he was the only man they had ever met who genuinely felt no fear. However, surely his subordinates were intimidated. Robertson must have been dissatisfied with the reaction time: he eventually said over the radio, "Conform and follow me," and took his tank to Point 144. Chadwick's group reached near Point 174 at 1715 hours, except Palmer's tank, whose engine seized up, due to the prior 88-mm strike.[7] Thus, Chadwick's group was down to seven Churchills.[8] Robertson's tank makes eight, although all of the war diaries and Joss' accounts ignore his contribution, so perhaps he eschewed taking hull-down positions himself, and stayed in the gulley.

Assuming that the Churchills headed directly for Point 174, they would have run for about 350 yards (320 m) down a gentle slope before reaching the bottom of the intervening saddle. This part of their journey was obscured by some 76-mm smoke shells fired by Joss' tank. From there they faced another 1,100 yards (1,000 m) of steady gentle climb to the summit. They probably erred left, where friendly infantry could be seen. Moreover, they should have wanted to travel to the left of a slight ridge leading up to Point 174. The more they erred right, the more their journey would have lengthened before they hit the main ridge, and the more exposed they would have been to the unsecured right flank.

The 7th Troop was probably the last troop to reach Point 174. It had been the first in Chadwick's group to Point 151. There, it was on the left of his line, so was the last to reach Point 144, and must have been the last to cross Point 144. By then, the 7th was the only complete troop in Chadwick's group, probably because it had stayed in reserve, out of sight, behind the hills, while 6th and 8th Troops took the risks and the casualties. Alan Gilmour was one of the drivers in 7th Troop. Writing four decades later, his account does not recall the move to 144, but does recall the charge up to Point 174. One part of his story seems most relevant to the start of his advance from Point 144:

> My commander wonders why again and again I pull "Titan" violently off course, not knowing that sometimes only a rifle feebly held above the long grass, visible to me at the last moment, prevents the tank from crushing a stricken infantryman…

More reported Panzers

If Chadwick had erred left of the slight ridge between Point 144 and Point 174, he would have remained visible to Joss throughout, at a distance of 700 yards (650 m), at shortest. The distance between them would have approached 1,000 yards (900 m) once Chadwick reached his likely objective – the intersection of the slight ridge and Point 174. At most, Chadwick would be about 275 yards (250 m) to the east of Tiger 131's reported location, although he would not have been able to see it, due to the height of the intervening summit. He would have oriented mostly north-eastwards, given the line of the crest at this point and the infantry positions.

Chadwick left no account of his own, and never corresponded with the veterans association, so we rely on Joss' hearsay. Joss himself could not see the other side of Point 174. According to Joss' account, Chadwick spotted five tanks (which he identified as Panzer IVs), side on, about 400 yards (366 m) away. Joss suggests that enemy tanks became visible as "Chadwick came up to the ridge of 174," and that they were "advancing along a ridge to the crest of 174," in column. If these tanks were real, they would have been heading towards Tiger 131, which was about the same distance away. Their route would have been invisible except to Chadwick, looking east of Point 174.

Chadwick's gunner opened fire with his two-pounder, then the next four Churchills took positions from which they also could open fire (with six-pounder guns). Chadwick's gunner fired 18 rounds in one minute, and claimed 12 hits,

---

7. Palmer's engine had seized up for want of cooling water. Later investigation found that a fragment from the 88-mm projectile that had burst underneath the belly had passed through the drainage cap in the floor of the engine compartment and damaged the tap controlling the circulation of the water.

8. Joss reported eight remaining after Palmer's loss, presumably by counting Norville's broken tank. The only surviving copy of his report (in the war diary held by the National Archives) shows a pencil strike through the Arabic number "8." As noted elsewhere, Joss made a habit of under-counting his own losses and over-counting the enemy's.

which "split open" one of the tanks, to quote Joss. Two minutes after opening fire, Chadwick claimed that all five tanks were hit, of which three were destroyed. The 142nd RAC recorded at least two destroyed by Chadwick's group.

However, these were probably amongst the six dummies identified in the same spot the next day. No Panzer IVs were reported as found on Point 174 after the battle. On 9th April, the North Irish Horse experienced a similar situation while operating on the northern side of the Medjerda valley, looking eastwards: a squadron commander went forward on foot and identified eight Tigers in hull-down positions, amongst a larger number of Panzer IIIs and Panzer IVs, but the supposed Tigers never fired or moved, despite being engaged by six Churchill tanks and indirect artillery. The number of dummies increased in that area during April. On 19th April, in the same valley, Allied aircraft bombed around 25 tanks, which intelligence analysts estimated as possibly Tigers (more than real Tigers operating in Tunisia). The next day, the same analysts decided they were probably dummies, when aircraft claimed 50 in the same place. Allied soldiers should have been aware that both sides deployed dummy tanks: the British had deployed dummy tanks in Tunisia since November to distract enemy aircraft; and in mid-April both Americans and British deployed hundreds of dummies to obscure the transfer of their armoured divisions northwards.

Joss' report claims that the six supposed Panzers on Point 174 "took evasive action and sought ground for cover," but he was not in a position to see them. Significantly, Joss noted that "they did not attempt to fire."

Gilmour helped to write the B Squadron's reconstructed diary (1947), with one statement on this part of the attack: "pressing on towards 174, the tanks are faced with opposition from Panzers and, racing forward, engage them on the move." Gilmour did not produce his own account until the 1980s, which seems to conflate later, more distant fire:

> We advance down the slope of 151 [144] and enemy tanks come out to meet us. In a tank versus tank duel, crews are toiling as they have never toiled before. An enemy tank presents a broadside target; every Churchill in our formation opens up, sending round after round screaming at it and battering it to destruction.

Probably Tiger 131 had been abandoned before Chadwick's group advanced on Point 174. Tiger 131 was never struck side-on by any tank's main armament, so was not amongst the five claimed by Chadwick's group. If Chadwick arrived on Point 174 before Tiger 131, then Tiger 131 would have been advancing to its final position, still out of sight of Chadwick on the other side of the summit. Likely, Tiger 131 had been disabled before Chadwick moved to Point 174, and that is why he felt confident about his chosen position.

Distant fire

Joss noted that Chadwick's group received incoming direct fire two minutes after Chadwick opened fire. This fire must have come from tanks or towed guns already positioned on a slight crest – 1,600 yards (1,500 m) north-east of Point 174, ready for any Allied tanks to top Point 174. Probably the dummies were arranged to attract fire from any tanks that crested Point 174, thereby revealing thmselves to the real defenders. Any Tiger amongst the weapons on the intervening crest should have stayed there, to continue the engagement at a range that only the Germans could win. Perhaps some tanks came down the track from Montarnaud to take hull-down positions behind this crest. Indeed, a burnt-out Tiger would be identified on the enemy side of this crest, after the Allied offensive on 6th May, although it might have been abandoned any day up to then, while escaping attacks in Gab-Gab Gap (see Chapter 12). Given the normal depth of German defences, probably other tanks or guns were in Montarnaud – less than 3,000 yards (2,700 m) from the summit of Point 174.

Alan Gilmour's memory, forty years later, continues to conflate the near dummies with the distant real Panzers:

> Inside "Titan" it is a degree hotter than hell. With every round fired, clouds of dust obscure the driving compartment. Every time the 6-pounder fires two feet above my driving hatch, the goggles jump on my nose and I experience the sensation of being hit on the head with a mallet. The roar of the tank's engine is drowned by louder noises so that its behaviour has to be gauged by the instrument panel, and yet I am loath to take my eyes for an instant from periscope or visor. Dimly the festoon lamps show my co-driver, sweat pouring from his face, eye glued to the telescopic sight of his gun…The waking nightmare goes on. Tiger tanks open up with 88s. From oblique, line-ahead progression we sweep parallel with the German armour, and since in this position we present good targets, we move fast. Firing our guns as rapidly as they can be loaded, we advance, throwing everything we have got at the Panzers. The 88s are doing devil's work, however. The tank ahead of "Titan" receives a direct hit, and two of the crew are instantly killed. With guns silenced, it crawls to cover, and a survivor pulls himself out of the fighting chamber; even as he does so, a second shell hits the turret, and his headless trunk falls down inside.

This stricken tank must be one of the two remaining tanks in 6th Troop that Joss reported as perforated by an 88-mm projectile, killing the loader and wounding the commander. In his letter to his commander, he recorded a write-off that might be the same tank: one shot split the 6-pounder's muzzle; another perforated the turret and wrecked the interior, including the power traverse.

A separate projectile nearly hit another commander – presumably Chadwick, who ordered withdrawal down into the saddle between Point 174 and Point 144. Gilmour had already backed his tank up to the crest, as ordered by his tank commander, in order to benefit from the extra protection of the engine:

> Surviving tanks maintain fire from hull-down positions, but we in "Titan" are too exposed, and shells fall close on each side. My commander gives the order to reverse, forgetting our gun is traversed to the rear, and we have our backs to the enemy lines. As I reverse, the tank mounts the crest of the hill in full view of the German guns.

After "Titan" was driven forward, it became the last of four survivors to reach the gulley between Point 174 and Points 144 and 151. The last two tanks to reach the crest (the tanks at the rears of 6th and 8th Troops respectively) never rallied. Joss presumed they were still searching for hull-down positions when the others withdrew. Indeed, after the battle they would be found knocked out.[9] Thus, only Chadwick's tank and the three tanks of 7th Troop survived to join a later attempt on Point 174 (at least the fourth attempt, including yesterday). He had lost six tanks since Point 151.

In the gulley

Joss claimed that while he was watching Chadwick's fight on Point 174, he belatedly decided that the rest of the squadron should take hull-down positions on Point 174. His account is unreliable, but he claimed only one loss on Point 151, leaving him with seven; Chadwick brought four back from Point 174 into the gulley, so the maximum that B Squadron could muster for another assault on Point 174 would have been eleven.

Gilmour remembered struggling to follow another tank on the track, which suggests that Chadwick's tanks were in column, perhaps in an effort to avoid landmines or the steepest parts of the slope. However, "Titan's" right (offside) track detonated double-stacked landmines. These probably had been buried especially deep so that they would not be triggered until several tanks had passed over. The blast carried away two wheel-units and the associated track, buckled the belly plate behind the driver's seat, bent his toolbox and tools out of shape, and destroyed the gear-change box, although nobody was hurt. We know the damage, cause, and location because "Titan" was one of two Churchills later recorded by the recovery team of 48th RTR as lost between Point 151 and Point 174. It was found at the bottom of the descent from Point 151, where the road/track crosses a wadi.

The crew of "Titan" dismounted before a Churchill came alongside to its left. This was Captain Rand's tank, which was leading the rest of the squadron from Point 151. Joss' accounts do not admit this, but Rand had already lost a Churchill I, with a two-pounder in the turret, and a howitzer in the hull: it was found days later by mechanics behind the crest of Point 151, with two wheels and associated track shot away, presumably by Tiger 131. Rand was now riding a Churchill IV taken from the 9th Troop commander, who must have walked back to Point 101.

Rand asked angrily why "Titan" was out of column. Despite being pointed to the offside damage, he continued on, but detonated mines ten yards away, which blew Gilmour and the machine-gunner through their hatches back into their seats. Rand's tank was a write-off ("Titan" was not): double-stacked mines wrecked the driver's compartment, all hydraulic pipes and gear rods, and the radio in the turret's rear. Rand found the turret traverse jammed, so ordered the crew to dismount. Then he discovered that the driver was still unconscious in his compartment, so Rand intercepted a passing Universal Carrier and added his driver to the patients therein. Rand ordered his crewmen to evacuate the tank's machine-guns, while he went to find the commander of the Foresters. Both crews decided to walk back 8 miles (13 km) towards Medjez, during which the gunner of "Titan" was wounded by mortar fire. After the battle, engineers lifted 13 mines from around the two tanks, some of which were between "Titan's" tracks. Gilmour was told that one landmine was configured to detonate the rest.

Meanwhile, Pye told Rand that tanks must remain on Point 174 all night in support of the infantry. Rand went to find the remaining tank of 9th Troop, which was following his. Rand ordered it to replenish from his own tank and to occupy Point 174, presumably for the night. Then Rand must have walked back to Point 151. Joss' typed report admits no doubts about Rand, but his private letter to his unit commander had reported Rand as injured with a "sprained ankle," "shaken up," the unit's "first captain out of battle," and left in charge of recovering and repairing tanks.

Point 174 again

The three tanks of 10th Troop approached the crest of Point 174 without mishap, by staying turret down. Sergeant Cummin must have been standing with his head above the crest when he claimed to spot a Tiger 500 yards away, stationary, and apparently abandoned. This was likely one of the dummies, given the range.

---

9. The last tank of 6th Troop was knocked out on Point 174 but did not burn. Under fire from small arms and mortars, the gunner (Trooper Nicoll) brought three wounded infantrymen back to its turret for shelter, treated them with the tank's first-aid kit, and reported their position to other infantry, for which he was awarded the Military Medal.

Suspicious of its use by observers directing the mortar fire, Cummin repositioned his tank to fire, when an 88-mm shot from the next crest punched in the hull machine-gun mounting, killed the co-driver, broke the gunner's leg, and jammed the turret. Cummin and the loader lifted the gunner and laid him behind the turret, then Cummin climbed into the driver's seat. He found the transmission stuck in reverse (presumably the driver was already backing up at time of impact), so he drove the tank backwards for 400 yards into the bottom of the gulley. (The hydraulic brakes were leaking slightly, although not enough to prevent driving, when mechanics reached it two days later.) Cummin went to Lieutenant Kingsford to point out the enemy gun. Kingsford directed his gunner to suppress it with machine-gun fire (presumably he had run out of 57-mm HE shells or never received any). Kingsford then grew anxious about being exposed too long while trying to correct the gunner on to the target. He took a turret-down position, and tried to fire his Bren light-machine-gun from its top, but had trouble with the feed from the 100-round magazines.

Joss must have been bringing up the rear, but did not report his own movements and was clearly out of touch with his squadron. The only surviving explanation is from his typed report, not his private letter:

> I went forward onto 174 with 9th and 10th Troops, but, owing to the fact that it was now getting too dark to observe, and I was not in contact with all my remaining tanks by wireless and therefore had not a clear idea of the numbers I then had, I ordered all tanks back to 151, where I thought I could rally and regroup the squadron and remain in a counter-attack role until orders to withdraw came through. I therefore returned to 151 and tried to get through to the CO [Robertson], but, although I tried for 20 minutes and called up every other station I could think of, I could not find out what was happening, nor get orders to withdraw. In about half an hour I did hear a faint call from a station I took to be 145th RAC on our extreme left, that they knew no more than me.

Withdrawal

Only five fight-capable tanks of 48th RTR reached the safe side of Point 151. Joss got there first. Chadwick returned the way he had come – through the gulley between Point 174 and Point 144, where he took Palmer's seized tank under tow; he towed it around the corner of Point 151, but it became too burdensome while crossing a ditch – 1,100 yards (1,000 m) south-west of Point 151. It would not be recovered further for another three days, after engineers had cleared the area of mines. Chadwick stopped his tank next to Joss, then they both dismounted to confer. They agreed for Joss to stay at his radio, awaiting higher orders, while Chadwick went on foot to establish the squadron's condition. Rand reported the remaining tank of 9th Troop on Point 174. Chadwick eventually met Kingsford, who reported that he had left his other tank of 10th Troop around Point 174. Thus, five tanks were counted as operational, although three would turn out to be not battleworthy. The 142nd RAC claimed ten surviving tanks.

The 142nd RAC war diary recorded that all surviving tanks withdrew at 1800 hours – "the position on 174 having been stabilized." The forward rally point was behind the crest of Point 151, where the track descends south-west of the 140-metre contour. At 1830 hours, Maxwell (25TB) ordered Robertson to meet at the other Point 101 (on the highway). Presumably Robertson took his own tank, because the 145th RAC lent a tank to the rump HQ left behind on Kat Zralb for the night.

At 1900 hours, the liaison officer from the Sherwood Foresters joined Robertson to relate that the infantry would need tank support to hold the crest overnight, so the 15 tanks on the forward rally point remained there without replenishment, under inaccurate fire from mortars – later, the explosives were joined by incendiary shells. The 145th RAC's composite squadron remained to the north, until its return to Kat Zralb at 2000 hours for replenishment.

After Chadwick had walked around discovering B Squadron's condition, he walked back to the farm at Kat Zralb, without reporting to Joss, presumably hoping to report to Robertson. Just before Kat Zralb, he ran into Kingsford, who was towing Cummin's tank. Chadwick next came across Maxwell, to whom he reported that four tanks of B Squadron were capable of helping Point 174 (he was ignoring Joss' close-support tank). Maxwell agreed for B Squadron to withdraw and to revert by morning to 24th Guards Brigade (on the left/north of 145th RAC). The time then was 2300 hours.

Meanwhile, Joss spent most of the dark hours in his turret with the Padre (Captain Scott Gardiner), who had been walking around the dead of all units under enemy fire. Joss was worried about anti-personnel mines, so persuaded him into the tank, where the six men shared bully beef and whiskey. About 2330 hours, Joss set off for the farm, walking within the tank tracks. Seeing no tanks there, he assumed that he had missed the order to withdraw. Back at his tank, his radio operator informed him that Chadwick had radioed a report from Kingsford's tank. Joss then ordered his squadron to withdraw. He shouted the same to Sergeant Cornish, who was commanding Chadwick's tank, but as they were moving off it detonated an anti-personnel mine that blew fragments or shrapnel into Cornish's head: he died before he reached the aid post. The running tanks rallied at Kat Zralb by 0130 hours. They needed to withdraw through the wrecks and minefields in the dark for another 3 miles (5 km) to their assembly area behind Snake Ridge, which they reached at 0230 hours.

Lyne could not obtain any orders (the various excuses of the day included: failing electrical batteries, distance, and enemy jamming), so, at 0030 hours, he ordered his ten tanks back to the Point 101 on the highway. Along the way, Lyne was met by Robertson, who ordered them back to the forward rally point, and to be ready to return to the crest of Point 151 at first light. Replenishment and maintenance were completed at the forward rally point by 0200 hours.

Outcomes

Joss wrote his letter to his unit commander (Gerry Brooks: temporarily commanding 21TB HQ) after he reached Snake Ridge at 0230 hours: he stated that the "attack was entirely successful and lasted 12 hours," which exaggerates both the success and the duration. Yet he complained that he was too weak to fulfill orders to repeat the attack.

> Although I can only put four tanks into battle at 0500 hours or six plus my tank at 0900 hours, as I write this, they [2nd Infantry Brigade] are trying to include me in another attack at dawn tomorrow!

After the tanks had been replenished and maintained, he realized that only two were battleworthy. He admitted this fact in his typed report, but even here he was disingenuous: he made no mention of the five write-offs, but claimed that ten were "damaged" and none was "destroyed." John Mennell (acting commander of 48th RTR, while Gerry Brooks was at 21TB) next wrote in his diary (26th April) that "B Squadron were in action the other day and lost ten tanks." Joss estimated the period of recovery as four to five days, although B Squadron (1947) admitted ten days.

In his letter, Joss wrote 13 tanks lost from his squadron, although he corrected the number to 16, after he realized that three of the five moving tanks were not battleworthy. The 48th RTR war diarist chose to record 15, presumably by counting only the Churchill IVs, rather than the Churchill I close-support tank that was damaged.[10] Joss was in the surviving close-support tank; Chadwick was in the other HQ tank (probably a Churchill II, where the howitzer in the forward hull was replaced by a machine-gun). Thus, neither of the two fight-ready tanks mounted a six-pounder.

The 142nd RAC recorded that its own composite squadron retained ten tanks, while 48th RTR's B Squadron retained five, so they had lost 21 between them in their shared fight for Point 174. The 145th RAC recorded that its composite squadron lost two tanks, so the total Churchill losses for Gueriat el Atach add up to 23 on this day alone. At least five must have been knocked out by Tiger 131 from Point 174 (three on Point 144; at least two on Point 151), excluding the three of the previous day.

Officially, the 1st Battalion of the King's Shropshire Light Infantry and the 2nd Battalion of the Sherwood Foresters suffered 329 casualties that day. No casualties for the tank units are given in the official history, nor enemy casualties (Playfair, 1966, p. 437). The 142nd RAC did not report personnel losses. Joss reported seven men killed and another eight wounded in his squadron.[11] The 145th RAC reported two men killed.

Joss's letter to Brooks claimed: "few [enemy] infantry were killed as they showed little fight and were captured." The ten lines appended to 48th RTR's war diary changed this statement to "many were captured." The official history records that the ridge was "recaptured quite easily" although the infantry were "plagued by tanks, mortars and *Nebelwerfers* [rocket artillery] hidden in nearby fields of growing corns." (Playfair, 1966, p. 437)

Joss concluded his letter with a claim that a Tiger was "damaged", and five other German tanks were "destroyed," including at least two Panzer IIIs. As explained above, he probably conflated the six dummies that would be identified by 142nd RAC the next day. Significantly, his typed report concluded with no claims. The 142nd RAC's war diary never recorded any claims. The 145th RAC's war diarist reported only one enemy loss ("We destroyed a Mk. VI"), but this was probably hearsay. Only Tiger 131 was definitely knocked out on the 24th. Tiger 131's abandonment would not be confirmed until daylight by local troops, and would not be escalated up the chain of command for days.

---

10. On the night of 24-25th April, Joss recorded in his letter one Churchill I repairable within the unit, five Churchill IVs repairable within the unit, three (later six) Churchill IVs escalated to Army workshops, and four Churchill IVs written off; a fifth was written-off on 26th April. Joss specified the four write-offs as: one burnt out (not explained in any of the primary sources); Rand's Churchill IV; Cummin's Churchill IV; and the Churchill IV shot through the turret front and with its muzzle split. Contradictorily, Joss also described Cummin as saving his tank from write-off. On 26th April, mechanics drove it away, but wrote it off, presumably because the machine-gun mounting or the leaky hydraulic brakes were too time-consuming to repair. Probably the fifth write-off is the tank of Chadwick's group that was penetrated on the climb up to Point 174. Possibly more tanks were written off later, due to delays in recovery. For instance, the 48th RTR's recovery report explains that recovery personnel visited Point 144 first on 27th April, when they were driven off for a couple hours by enemy planes and mortars. Getting Norville's tank back to the leaguer took until 28th April. On that day, another two of the unit's tanks were recorded as impossible to recover due to mortar fire. The report on recovery efforts identified five of the six escalated to Army workshops, of which two had been disabled by landmines; one had lost two wheels and some track to an unidentified shot near the crest of Point 151; Palmer's running gear had been damaged by an 88-mm shot and his engine had seized; and Corporal Norville's tank had been hit through the left louvre and track by an 88-mm shot. The squadron nominally held 18 Churchills, so the loss rate (temporary and write-offs) ran to 89 percent. Thus, B Squadron's reconstructed war diary is wrong to report two-thirds. The five write-offs amount to a loss rate of 28 percent.

11. Four men were killed by 88-mm shots, apparently in two different tanks, given the way Joss grouped them in pairs. Additionally, two were killed by mortars, one by a landmine.

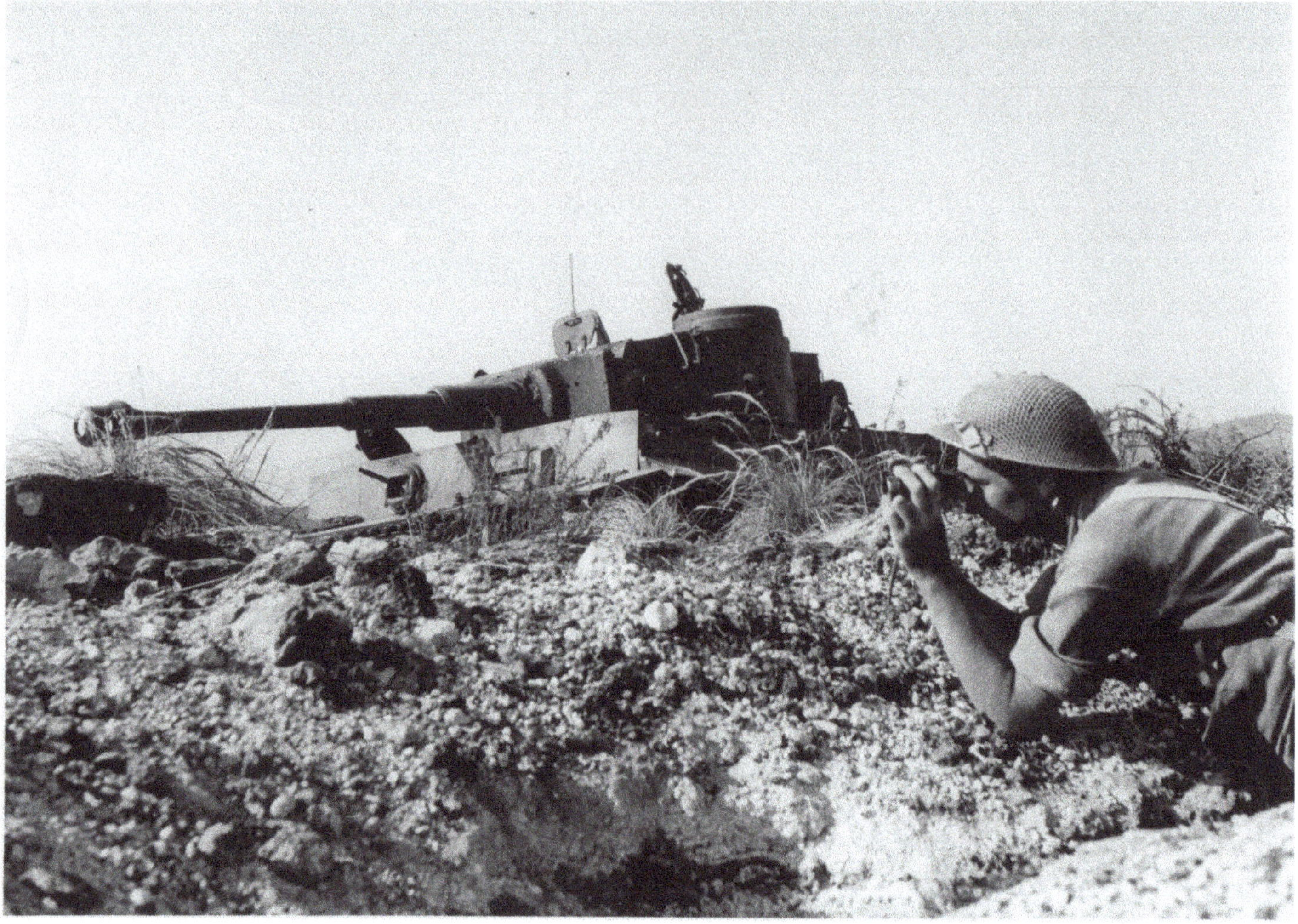

This is one of three photographs taken of Tiger 131 in its place of capture, probably on 26th April 1943, during the first visit by the Army Film & Photographic Unit. (The other two can be found on page 22, in the chapter describing Tiger 131's confrontation with British infantry.) Some infantry had pushed positions forward, but this soldier is occupying a trench to the south-western side of the summit, above the reverse slope, without line of sight on the forward slope. He is looking towards the north-western (left) flank, around Point 158, where artillery shells are bursting, as proven by a coincident moving picture. The roll of film was marked as "taken by Sgt. Wackett, 27.4.43." However, official photographs were dated when a roll of film was bagged for despatch. The negative was archived with the explanation: "Tiger tank captured by 2nd Battalion Sherwood Foresters after fighting west [actually: due east] of Medjez el Bab." A print was archived at STT with the caption: "One of our men observing enemy positions, the German Tiger is seen over the top of the trench."

THE DAILY SKETCH, TUESDAY, MAY 11, 1943.—Page 8

From a ridge captured in the advance on Tunis a British soldier watches the retreating enemy. Near by is one of Germany's much-vaunted monster "Tiger" tanks. It was knocked out by our gunners—using a German anti-tank gun which we had captured complete with ammunition.

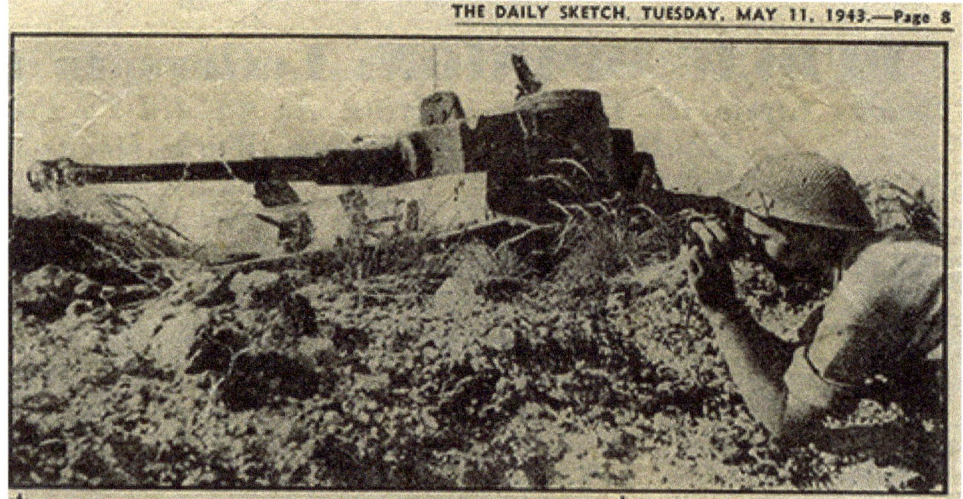

A clip was published on 11th May in the *Daily Sketch* newspaper, with the following caption: "From a ridge captured in the advance on Tunis, a British soldier watches the retreating enemy [*sic*]. Nearby is one of Germany's much-vaunted monster 'Tiger' tanks. It was knocked out by our gunners – using a German anti-tank gun which we had captured complete with ammunition."

CHAPTER 7

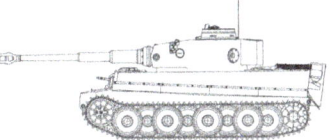

THE CONSOLIDATION OF POINT 174

The units involved at Gueriat el Atach spent up to ten days refitting, which ended on 4th May.[12] By then, the same units were making ready to assault from Point 174 eastwards, at the start of the decisive offensive towards Tunis, on 6th May.

The day after

On the night of Tiger 131's abandonment, the Germans were distracted southwards, when 4ID attacked through Peters Corner. The 4ID's left came up to Point 144, which then received more indirect fire and even dive bombers.

At 0430 hours, 25th April, the composite squadron from 145th RAC "returned to the front line [presumably Point 158], under constant mortar fire," as its war diarist recorded. By dawn, the composite squadron from 142nd RAC was in ready reserve (35 minutes notice) in the gulley between Points 151 and 174: "The squadron remained in position all the morning, being subjected to continuous fire from mortars and artillery." The Foresters' war diary for the day is bare: "Heavy shelling and mortaring all day."

The 2nd Sherwood Foresters spent a total of ten days on Point 174, under incessant indirect fire that discouraged any movement outside their entrenchments. The battalion's commander did not want tanks, which drew enemy fire. At midday, somebody radioed to 142nd RAC's acting commander (Major S.D.G. Robertson) that they were under fire from a Panzer on the other side of Point 174, and that the Churchills would need to intervene or the infantry could not hold the hill. The squadron commander (Major F.G.L. Lyne) denied any knowledge of this tank; he enquired at an O.P. manned by the Foresters, who confirmed no Panzer. Lyne reported to Robertson, who repeated the infantry's claim. Lyne prepared to go forward on foot, when an infantry officer found him to declare that the infantry had suffered 40% casualties and he needed to coordinate a plan for the tanks to help. Lyne sent two troops, but they did not find any Panzer: perhaps the infantry's messages had meant to indicate a wrecked or dummy Panzer from where an enemy FOO was suspected of observing the indirect fire.

Lyne took a separate pair of troops around the right of Point 174. Sergeant Brighty drew attention to six tanks, which proved to be dummies. Anti-tank guns opened fire from near Montarnaud, sending the troops running back into the gulley, where they received heavy indirect fire.

At 1500 hours, A Squadron from 48th RTR rotated with the composite squadron. This squadron's only action so far had been its bloody failure to dislodge German raiders, including a Tiger, from Djebel Djaffa, on the 21st (Newsome 2020d). Peter Gudgin was one of its subalterns. He had been evacuated with a head wound. After medical evaluation, per standard procedure, he was passed to the reinforcement unit, which was preparing new or recovered tanks and crewmen. In some of his accounts, he claimed to receive a new tank on 22nd April, although he never claimed to be part of B Squadron, which was the only part of his unit engaged on 24th April. Gudgin was probably still in "shock," as post-traumatic stress was known at the time, for which the normal treatment was to be left out of battle for a while. This helps to explain why his only assignment since Djebel Djaffa was as liaison officer to the Foresters on 25th April.

> We took up positions on the reverse slope of Point 174 and I reported to the Foresters' CO in his command post dugout. He, however, curtly told me to take my tank away and dig my own foxhole. There seemed to be nothing for it but to move some 30 yards away down the slope, although obviously this would make liaison very difficult, particularly in view of the heavy mortar fire then being directed at us. Having moved the tank, I quickly grabbed the shovel off the engine deck and scraped frantically at the stony ground until I was more or less below ground surface level. With two jumper leads connecting my headset to the tank's wireless set and my tank closed down against the heavy and constant mortar fire coming in, I lay there for some five hours without any communication from or with the Foresters' HQ. When at last we received the order from our Battalion HQ to pull out I mounted my tank thankfully and reversed down the hill at high speed and without saying goodbye to the Foresters. To give their CO his due, however, it later transpired that they had suffered heavy casualties in the attack, and he personally had been fired at, luckily without success, by B Squadron's tanks as he returned from reconnaissance in his carrier.

---

12. The exceptions were 145th RAC, and A Squadron of 48th RTR, which was put under command on 30th April for an attack across Gab-Gab Gap to the north of Point 174. They stayed on duty there until 4th May (see Chapter 12).

The other men of A Squadron stayed in their tanks, further back, safe from the mortar fire. The Squadron remained in ready reserve (effectively a quick reaction force) until 2000 hours, one hour after dark. On or about the next day,[13] Gudgin reported to the unit doctor, complaining of a blind spot in his right eye and general light sensitivity, which he attributed to flash or blast on 21st April. He was sent back to hospital. There he admitted to "depression" over his own injury and the death of Lieutenant Alan Lott (Newsome 2020d), which led swiftly to his evacuation to Britain.

The second day after

At 1500 hours, Lyne's composite squadron had withdrawn behind Point 151. At 1730 hours, it withdrew to the Point 101 on the highway for replenishment. By dawn on 26th April, a separate composite squadron from 142nd RAC, this time under Major F.W. Roper, went forward to Point 174. The orders received during the night (presumably from 3rd Brigade) were to head left of the road/track in support of the Shropshire Light Infantry on Point 158: the unit's reconnaissance officer and liaison officer reconnoitred positions overnight. However, the 25TB HQ countermanded the orders, and redirected the squadron right of the road/track in support of the Foresters.

The commander of the Foresters asked Roper to take positions on Point 151 rather than draw fire on to Point 174. Roper stood by all day, with frequent rumours of Panzers that never materialized. The Foresters' war diary recorded: "Re-adjustment of co[mpan]y positions. Position now firmly held. Enemy shelling continues but with less intensity."

The remaining days on Point 174

The 25TB was diverted from 26th April to prepare attacks on the hills to the north-west, while parts of 21TB were attached to those efforts to the north-west or held to the south in counter-attack role. Throughout, both brigades were simultaneously trying to rebuild their capacity in readiness for the final offensive on 6th May.

The 48th RTR's recovery efforts were driven off Point 144 on 27th April by dive-bombers and mortars (although the infantry stayed on the hill). The unit gave up on 28th April, with two of its tanks still outstanding, due to more mortar fire and news of enemy tanks massing near Massicault (about 14 miles or 22 km by highway from the unit's harbour at Banana Ridge). On 29th April, yet another unit of 21TB (12th RTR) got sucked into the fight to the north-west, losing at least 35 tanks and 82 men, all within sight or sound of the hills of Gueriat el Atach. The 48th RTR's acting commander (John Mennell) wrote in his diary:

> Did a recce today on Pt. 151. Certain amount of carnage and a little mortaring. A dive bomb attack was in progress on 1st Div. area. Too close for comfort. Enemy air seems to have increased recently. For reasons given above attack is going slowly and at great expense.

Fighting continued in the neighbourhood until 29th April. The Foresters were not relieved until early on 3rd May. The area was still on the front until 6th May, when Hill 174 was part of the start-line for the largest Western Allied offensive to date, leading within days to Tunis and victory in Tunisia. The local assault was by 4th Indian Division, supported by both tank brigades: all the same units that had fought for Hill 174 on 24th April were in the lead.

(Overleaf, lower) This print (dated 6th May 1943) was stamped by the War Office as an official photograph, and by the Press & Censorship Bureau of the Ministry of Information as passed for publication, then distributed to the Enemy AFV Section of STT, at the same time as other prints were distributed to the press. Most images in STT's archives were obtained by the same unprivileged process: in other words, the Army's own photographers were disconnected from the Army's repository of intelligence on foreign tanks. This print was punched with holes for filing, without any caption. Likely, it was not used officially further. The Section sometimes mounted prints on card for instructional purposes, but no prints of Tiger 131 have survived in this condition. Lidderdale obtained a print for his own album; in the 1970s, Peter Gudgin painted and typed over his caption to claim that: Tiger 131 was knocked out by A Squadron, 48th RTR; the man wearing the beret, with his back to the camera, is the commander of 48th RTR; the Dingo and Churchill IV tank are from 48th RTR; and the soldiers are from the East Surreys Regiment. These claims could be true only if this photograph was taken on 22nd April at Djebel Djaffa. However, he did not amend the place (Point 174) or provide a date. He was not present. The 8th Argyll & Sutherland Highlanders had relieved the Foresters on 3rd May. Probably some of the personnel here are from the Army Film & Photographic Unit. The soldier on the tank's rear appears to be pointing a camera or perhaps a compass north-eastwards.

13. In one account, he dated his admittance to hospital on 2nd May, before he returned to the Tank Delivery Squadron, after which he saw 7th Armoured Division pass by during its transfer from 8th Army on the south-eastern front to 1st Army on the north-western front. In fact, the 7AD made the transfer from 30th April to 2nd May, so he must have been admitted to hospital earlier than 2nd May – probably on 26th April. Moreover, in private letters to strangers that joined his unit after his departure he introduced himself by explaining that he had been evacuated to Britain at the end of April. None of his accounts claim that he saw Tiger 131 in its place of capture. In another account, Gudgin claimed that he was still with the Tank Delivery Squadron, and unassigned to any unit, on 6th May (the first day of the final offensive), and was near the open area used by 104th Army Tank Workshops when Tiger 131 was towed in. Further, he claimed, he was so awed that he sketched it into a letter to his father, but he never produced this letter.

(Left) On 6th May, the 2nd Army Film & Photographic Unit returned to record the first day of the decisive offensive: one axis started from Point 174 and was still visible on the ridges eastwards. By then, Tiger 131 had been guided backwards (likely in neutral gear, with gravity) for 200 yards from the crest to almost the track. The line of travel is consistent with its position on the crest, facing south-eastwards to Point 151. Its gun is slightly traversed to right of centre. Presumably it was wanted below Point 174 so that investigation would be less visible to the enemy. Some contents were discarded on the ground, posed on the front of the tank, or carried away.

Escalating Tiger 131

Their damaged Churchills were still being recovered to the Army workshops that day. Hours after the attackers had advanced from Point 174, the same workshops sent a team to inspect Tiger 131 for recovery. In order for a recovery team to arrive on 6th May, somebody must have realized earlier the significance of Tiger 131 and the prospects for recovering it, once Axis artillery would be driven out of range. The trigger might have been Captain Noel Gee of 22nd Field Artillery Regiment, who took over a forward observation post next to Tiger 131. On 4th May, he wrote in his diary:

> Spent the day at OP beside a Mk. VI on Pt. 174 studying Montarnaud. Rumours of the BIG ATTACK. [The] 8th Army begins to arrive: 4th Indian Div. and masses of artillery.

Gee knew of no other Tiger in Allied hands, so he sketched the tank, and sent the drawing back to his Battery for escalation up the chain of command.

On 5th May, the acting commanders of the Churchill units were told of their roles in the coming offensive. Some were brought up to an observation post on or about Point 174, which would be the sight for 21TB's advanced HQ. Mennell (48th RTR) was one of them:

> I spent an hour looking at our immediate objectives from a cleverly camouflaged OP. This OP overlooked Montarnaud where the enemy has a considerable number of mortars. I was again struck by the amazing way the battlefield is totally quiet when there is no actual fighting going on. From this position I could see the B Squadron tanks which had been knocked out by the Tiger on Pt. 174. Went back to our forward area. All was quiet for a time but then the Hun must have spotted some dust as he shelled us in a spasmodic way for about four hours.

Recovering Tiger 131

At some point, the escalation reached the right person at 1st Army HQ, who ordered Major A. Douglas Lidderdale of the 104th Army Tank Workshop to recover Tiger 131. On site, Lidderdale met with the V Corps' Deputy Director of Mechanical Engineering (DDME), so perhaps the latter was the necessary node in the authorization.

The offensive started hours before dawn on the 6th. Lidderdale arrived some hours after. He took assistance from Lieutenant Reg Whatley and Assistant Quarter-Master Sergeant Shaw of 25th Tank Brigade's workshop. Whatley inspected the vehicle for booby traps, before all climbed inside. The fluid levels were adequate, although water was low. Lidderdale recorded in his notepad and first report (19th September 1943) the tank's tactical number (131), turret number (230639), and hull number (250122). Whatley told him that the Tiger had been disabled by a Churchill tank from 145th RAC, 25th Tank Brigade. (The 145th was the only unit from 25TB involved on 24th April, and Whatley represented 25TB!) Lidderdale wrote this information in his notepad and subsequent report. He recorded the location as "Point 174 on the Medjez-el-Bab to Montarnaud Road" where it had "been immobilized in battle."

On 7th May, Lidderdale brought up a Caterpillar D8 tracked tractor to tow Tiger 131. The tractor towed Tiger 131 along the track south-westwards, over the crest where it had met its enemies, and another 8 miles (13 km) to Medjez-el-Bab, then south for more than 3 miles (5 km) down a secondary road nicknamed "Red Cap Alley." The D8 had towed Tiger 131 for more than 11 miles (18 km) to the flat area being used by the 104th Army Tank Workshop.

The same area had been fought over during the German spoiling attack of 20th to 21st April (see Newsome 2020d). The site was otherwise unremarkable; Tiger 131 arrived unceremoniously, like any of the Churchill tanks that were dumped hereabouts for repair.

Reference List

Note: All primary sources discussed in the text can be found in the Tank Museum Archives and respective national archives. The following list includes all the secondary sources cited in this volume.

Aberger, Heinz-Dietrich (1994). Die 5. (lei.)/21. Panzer Division in NordAfrika, 1941-1943, Reutlingen: Preussicher Militär-Verlag.
Anderson, Kenneth, A.N. (1943). Operations in North West Africa from 8th November 1942 to 13th May 1943, 7th June 1943, reprinted in: Supplement to The London Gazette, No. 37,779, 5th November 1946, p. 5449-5464.
Arnim, Hans-Jürgen von (1951). "Tunisian Campaign," United States Army Europe HQ, Historical Division, Foreign Military Studies Branch, C-094.
Atkinson, Rick (2002). An Army at Dawn: The War in North Africa, 1942-1943, New York: Henry Holt.
Barclay, C.N. (1953). The History of the Duke of Wellington's Regiment, 1919-1952, London: William Clowes & Sons.
Beckett, Frank (1986). Algiers to Austria with the 1st and 8th Armies, Grimsby, England: Graphic Press.
Bender, Roger James, and George A. Petersen (1993). Hermann Göring: From Regiment to Fallschirmpanzerkorps, Atglen, PA: Schiffer.
Bennett, Ralph (1989). Ultra and Mediterranean Strategy, New York: William Morrow & Company
Blake, R.L.V. ffrench (1962). A History of the 17th/21st Lancers, 1922-1959, London: Macmillan.
Blumenson, Martin (1961). Breakout and Pursuit: European Theater of Operations, Washington, DC: Office of the Chief of Military History.
Boscawen, Robert (2010). Armoured Guardsmen: A War Diary, June 1944-April 1945, Barnsley, England: Pen & Sword.
Bradley, Omar N. (1951). A Soldier's Story, New York: Henry Holt.
Bürker, Ulrich (1947). "Commitment of the 10th Panzer Division in Tunisia," United States Army Europe HQ, Historical Division, D-174.
Calvocoressi, Peter (1980). Top Secret Ultra, New York: Pantheon Books.
Carrell, Paul [Paul Karl Schmidt] (1958). Die Wüsten Füchste, Hamburg: Henri Nannen Verlag.
Carver, Michael (1989). Out of Step: Memoirs of a Field Marshal, London: Hutchinson.
Cook, Hugh (1970). The North Staffordshire Regiment: The Prince of Wales's: The 64th/98th Regiment of Foot, London: Leo Cooper.
Cox, Richard (1995). Tiger Without a Home: The United States Ordnance Museum's Panzerkampfwagen VI, Aberdeen, Maryland: US Army Ordnance Museum Foundation.
Daniell, David Scott (1955). Regimental History: The Royal Hampshire Regiment, Volume 3, 1918-1954, Aldershot: Gale & Polden.
Dean, C.G.T. (2003). The Loyal Regiment (North Lancashire), 1919-1970, Doncaster, England: D.P.&G. Military Publishers.
Eisenhower, Dwight D. (1948). Crusade in Europe, New York: Doubleday.
Evans, Bryn (2012). With the East Surreys in Tunisia, Sicily and Italy, 1942-1945, Barnsley, England: Pen & Sword.
Feist, Uwe, and Bruce Culver (1992). Panzerkampfwagen Tiger, Retford, England: Ryton.
Fletcher, David (1986). Tiger! The Tiger Tank: A British View, London: Her Majesty's Stationery Office.
Fletcher, David, David Willey, Mike Hayton, Mike Gibb, et al (2011)., Tiger Tank: Owner's Workshop Manual, Sparkford, England: Haynes.
Foley, C. John (1975). Mailed Fist, Saint Albans, England: Mayflower Books.
Gause, Alfred (1946). Military Operations Against American Troops in Africa, United States Army Europe HQ, Historical Division, Foreign Military Studies Branch, D-385
Guderian, Heinz (1952). Panzer Leader, trans. Constantine Fitzgibbon, London: Michael Joseph.
Gudgin, Peter, The Tiger Tanks, London: Arms and Armour, 1991.
– (1996). With Churchills to War: 48th Battalion Royal Tank Regiment at War 1939-45, Thrupp, England: Sutton Publishing.
Hammerton, John, ed. (1946). The Second Great War: A Standard History, 9 volumes, Waverley Book Company.
Hartmann, Bernd (2011). Panzers in the Sand: The History of Panzer-Regiment 5, Volume 2, 1942-1945, Barnsley, England: Pen & Sword.
Hartmann, Wilhelm (1975). "Schwere Panzer-Abteilung (Tiger) 501," in RACTM E2016.2021.
Hastings, Max (1984). Overlord: D-Day and the Battle for Normandy, London: Michael Joseph.
Hastings, RHWS (1950). The Rifle Brigade in the Second World War, 1939-1945, Aldershot: Gale & Polden.
Henderson, Jim (1958). 22 Battalion, The Official History of New Zealand in the Second World War, 1939-1945, Wellington: War History Branch.
Hinsley, F.H., Edward Eastaway Thomas, C.F.G. Ransom, and R.C. Knight (1981). British Intelligence in the Second World War: Its Influence on Strategy and Operations, Volume 2, London: Her Majesty's Stationery Office.
Howe, George F. (1954). The Battle History of the 1st Armored Division, Nashville, TN: The Battery Press.
– (1957). Northwest Africa: Seizing the Initiative in the West, United States Army in World II: Mediterranean Theater of Operations, Washington, DC: Office of the Chief of Military History, Department of the Army.
– (1980). American Signal Intelligence in Northwest Africa and Western Europe, Fort Mead, Maryland: National Security Agency.
Howze, Hamilton H. (1996). A Cavalryman's Story: Memoirs of a Twentieth-Century Army General, Washington: Smithsonian Institution Press.
Jentz, Thomas L. (1997). Germany's Tiger Tanks: Tiger I and II: Combat Tactics, Atglen, PA: Schiffer.
– (2001). Germany's Tiger Tanks: Tigers at the Front, Atglen, PA: Schiffer.
Jervois, W.J. (1953). The History of the Northamptonshire Regiment, 1934-1948, London: The Regimental History Committee.
Jones, R.V. (1978). Most Secret War: British Scientific Intelligence, 1939-1945, London: Hamish Hamilton.
Jordan, Philip (1943). Jordan's Tunis Diary, London: Collins.

King, James (2002). Farley: The Life of Farley Mowat, Toronto: Harper Perennial.
Kleine, Egon, and Volkmar Kühn (1976). Tiger: Die Geschichte einer legendären Waffe, 1942-1945. Stuttgart: Motorbuch Verlag.
Kurowski, Franz (1995). The History of the Fallschirmpanzerkorps Hermann Göring, David Johnston, tr., Winnipeg, Canada: J.J. Fedorowicz Publishing.
Lewin, Ronald (1978). Ultra Goes to War, London: Hutchinson.
Liddell Hart, Basil (1970). History of the Second World War, London: Cassell.
Macksey, Kenneth (1994). "A Tiger we never tamed," Sunday Times, 5th June 1994, p. 11.
Masters, John (1946). The Story of the 2nd Battalion The Sherwood Foresters, 1939-45, Aldershot: Gale & Polden.
Miles, Wilfrid (1961). The Gordon Highlanders, 1919-1945: Aberdeen: The University Press.
Montgomery, Bernard Law (1947). Normandy to the Baltic, London: Hutchinson.
Moore, Tony, and Raj Lakha (2007), eds. Tolley's Handbook of Disaster and Emergency Management: Principles and Practice, 3rd edition, Amsterdam: Elsevier.
Mowat, Farley (1992). My Father's Son: Memories of War and Peace, New York: Houghton Mifflin.
Newsome, Bruce Oliver (2020a). The Rise and Fall of Western Tanks, 1915-1945, Coronado, CA: Tank Archives Press.
- (2020b). PzKw. VI Tiger Tank: The Official Wartime Reports: Coronado, CA: Tank Archives Press.
- (2020c). The Tiger Tank and Allied Intelligence, Volume 1, Grosstraktor to Tiger 231, 1926-1943, Coronado: Tank Archives Press.
- (2020d). The Tiger Tank and Allied Intelligence, Volume 2, The Tunisian Tigers, 1943, Coronado, CA: Tank Archives Press.
- (2020e). The Tiger Tank and Allied Intelligence, Volume 3, Tiger 131: From Africa to Europe, Coronado, CA: Tank Archives Press.
- (2020f). The Tiger Tank and Allied Intelligence, Volume 4, Capabilities and Performance, Coronado, CA: Tank Archives Press.
Patton, George S. (1947). War As I Knew It, Boston: Houghton Mifflin.
Playfair, Ian S.O. (1966). The Mediterranean and Middle East, Volume 4, The Destruction of the Axis Forces in Africa, London: Her Majesty's Stationery Office.
Quarrie, Bruce (1978). Fallschirmpanzerdivision Hermann Göring, London: Osprey.
Restayn, Jean (2013). Tiger I in Action, 1942-1945, Paris: Histoire & Collections.
Roach, Peter (1982). The 8:15 to War: Memoirs of a Desert Rat, Leo Cooper.
Ruff, Volker (2015). Der Tiger, Volume 1, Shwere Panzerabteilung 501, Heathfield, England: Panzerwrecks.
Schneider, Wolfgang (1998). Tigers in Combat, Volume II, Winnipeg, Canada: J.J. Fedorowicz.
Schneider, Wolfgang (1995). Tigers in Combat, Volume I, Winnipeg, Canada: J.J. Fedorowicz.
Solarz, Jacek (2005). Tiger in Action, 1942-1943, Warsaw: Wydawnictwo Militaria.
Spielberger, Walter J. (1991). Tiger and King Tiger Tanks and Their Variants, Sparkford: Haynes [1987, Stuttgart: Motorbuch Verlag].
Spielberger, Walter J. (1994). Der Panzerkampfwagen Panther und seine Abarten, Militärfahrzeuge vol. 9, Stuttgart: Motorbuch.
Spielberger, Walter J., and Uwe Feist (1968). Panzerkampfwagen VI Tiger I & II Konigstiger, Berkeley, California: Feist Publications.
Trojca, Waldemar (2010). Technical and Operational History: Tiger, 1942-1943, Volume 1, Katowice, Poland: Model Hobby.
United States Military Academy (1947). The War in North Africa, Part 2, The Allied Invasion, West Point, NY: Author.
Värst, Gustav von (1947). "Operations of the 5th Panzer Army in Tunisia," United States Army Europe HQ, Historical Division, Foreign Military Studies Branch, D-001.
War Office (1942). AFV Field Pocket Book, Facsimile Edition, Coronado, CA: Tank Archives Press.
Weber, Friedrich (1948). "Battles of 334th Division and of Group Weber from the end of December 1942 to May 1943," US Army Europe HQ, Historical Division, D-215.
Werner, Christoph Wilhelm (1947). The Battles of the Hermann Göring Division in Tunisia from January to 12th May 1943, Foreign Military Studies Branch, D-085.
Williamson, Hugh (1951). The Fourth Division, 1939 to 1945, London: Newman Neame.
Winterbotham, F.W. (1975). The Ultra Secret, London: Weidenfeld & Nicolson.

Index

1st Army (British), 48n, 50, 53
1st Infantry Division (British), 7, 13, 15, 16, 44
10th Brigade, 15
104th Army Tank Workshop, 14, 35, 48, 50
12th Brigade (British), 15
12th RTR, 48
142nd RAC, 7-21, 33-36, 42, 44-46, 47-48
145th RAC, 7, 12, 15-17, 44-45, 47, 59
18th Army Group, 53
21st Tank Brigade, 7, 15, 45, 48
22nd Field Regiment, RA, 50
24th Guards Brigade, 7, 8, 12, 44
25-pounder gun: see Twenty-Five Pounder
25th Tank Brigade, 7, 13, 15-16, 44, 48, 50
3rd Brigade (British), 7, 10, 13, 15-16, 48
334th Division (German), 7
4th Infantry Division (British), 15, 47
48th RTR, 12-13, 10-19, 21, 33-34, 43-45, 48
501st Heavy Tank Battalion, 5
504th Heavy Tank Battalion, 5, 11, 12, 25
6th Armoured Division (British), 48
7th Armoured Division (British), 48
78th Division (British), 7
8th Army (British), 48, 50
805th Tank Destroyer Battalion, 27
81st Reconnaissance Battalion, 21, 28
88-mm L56 gun, 12-14, 34-35, 41-42, 44-45
Anderson, Kenneth, 39, 53
Anti-personnel mine, 9, 10, 44
Argyll and Sutherland Highlanders, 48
Army Film and Photographic Unit, 46, 48, 49, 53
Banana Ridge, 66, 8, 10, 16, 48, 51, 53
Bell, G.G., 16
Birkbeck A.E., 10, 13-15
Blagden, Willie, 18, 38, 53
Bouch, G.A., 8
Brighty, 47
Brooks, Gerry, 15, 45
Carrier, Bren Gun or Universal, 8, 10, 12, 15, 43
Carter, D.B. 8
Centrifugal air cleaner, 25, 29, 53
Chadwick, Neil R.M., 19, 33, 41-45
Chouigui, 7
Churchill tank, 7, 9-10, 12-13, 15-18, 25, 30, 33-35, 42-55, 48, 50-52, 54
Cooke, 39
Cornish, 44
Cripps, M.L., 48
Cummin, 43-45
Djebel Bou Mous (Grenadier Hill), 51
Djebel Djaffa (Point 381), 5, 6, 15, 16, 39, 47-48, 51
Djebel el Mourhra, 51
Djebel Hoka, 16
Djebel Touila, 51
Dodson, A.H., 12
Duke of Wellington's Regiment (The Dukes), 10, 14, 15, 19, 21
Dummy tanks, 7, 14, 17, 20, 21, 42, 43, 47
Feifel, Eugen, 25
Forrest, J.E., 10, 13
Fulbrook, E., 9, 12
Gardiner, Scott., 44
Gee, G.S., 48
Gee, Noel, 19, 23, 50
Gibson, D.B., 8
Gilmour, Alan, 16, 18-19, 41, 43, 53
Gordon Highlanders, 7, 10, 14, 33
Goubellat, 11, 16, 52
Gudgin, Peter, 6, 39, 47, 51
Gueriat el Atach, 6, 8, 11, 15, 18, 21, 26, 29, 32, 45, 47, 48
Hamilton, J.A., 6
Hawkins, E.W., 8
Hermann Göring Division, 7
Ivor-Moore, Thomas, 15
Joss, Cecil A. "Bill," 15-21, 33-34, 41-45
King George VI, 38
King's Shropshire Light Infantry, 15, 17, 45, 48
Kingsford, 44
Lidderdale, Douglas A., 35-38, 40, 48, 50
Lister, C.V.K., 13
Lott, Alan, 48
Loyal Regiment (North Lancashire), 7
Lyne, F.G.L., 10, 13, 15-17, 21, 45, 47, 48
M3 Tank Destroyer, 18, 20, 22, 24, 28, 33
MacCarthy, Jock, 19
Massicault, 48
Matthews, H.A.E., 15-16
Maxwell, R.H., 13, 15, 16, 44
Medjerda River, 7, 42
Medjez el Bab, 6-7, 14-17, 23, 43, 46, 50-54
Mennell, John, 15, 45, 48, 50
Middle East Command, 28
Ministry of Supply, 29, 53
Montarnaud, 6, 32, 33, 36, 42, 47, 50
Moore, Eric, 10, 14
Newnham, H.C.C., 42, 45-46, 48
Nicoll, 43
North Irish Horse, 42, 52
North Staffordshire Regiment, 7-10
Norville, 33, 41, 45
Oclee, H.D., 8
PaK 97/38 75-mm gun, 23-24, 34
Palmer, 34, 41, 44-45
Panzer III, 14, 24, 42, 45
Panzer IV, 10, 14, 21, 24, 41-42
Peters Corner, 15, 47
Point 101, Kat Zralb, 6, 11-12, 14-17, 32-36, 43-44
Point 101, near Snake Ridge, 6, 7, 14, 44, 45, 48
Point 104, 6-9, 12, 32-33
Point 144, 6-7, 10, 13, 17, 19, 21, 32-34, 41-45, 47-48
Point 151, 6-10, 13-14, 16-19, 21, 32-34, 41, 43-44, 48-49
Point 156, 51-52
Point 158, 6-8, 10, 12, 14, 15, 17-18, 32-33, 46-48
Point 166, 51
Point 168, 6, 8
Point 170, 8, 13, 18, 21, 32-33
Point 174, 6-10, 12-19, 21, 24, 26, 32-36, 41-45, 57-48, 50, 53
Point 187, 15
Pye, R.T.K., 19, 43
Rand, Maurice, 33, 34, 43-45
Red Cap Alley, 50
Reynolds, F.J., 16
Robertson, S.D.G., 10, 13-17, 33, 41, 44, 45, 47
Roper, F.W., 12-14, 48
Sandys-Clark, Wilward A., 9
School of Tank Technology, 28, 36, 38, 48
Scorpion Corner, 50-52
Scots Guards, 8
Sened, 12,, 50
Sfax, 13
Sherwood Foresters, 13-21, 23-24, 33, 43-48
Six-Pounder Gun, 12, 34, 39, 41, 42, 45
Snake Ridge, 6, 7, 14, 16, 17, 44
Technical intelligence, 5, 30
Tiger 131/731 of the 501st Battalion, 5, 7
Tiger 131 of the 504th Battalion, 5-7, 11-29, 32, 41-43, 45-50
Tiger 142 of the 504th Battalion, 11
Tiger 221/712 of the 501st Battalion, 5
Tiger 231 of the 501st Battalion, 5
Tiger 712 of the 501st Battalion, 5
Tiger 731 of the 501st Battalion, 5, 7
Tunis, 7, 10, 15, 39, 46-48, 51-53
Twenty-Five Pounder Gun, 7
Two-Pounder Gun, 33-34, 41, 43
Tyrrell, G.H.P., 16, 17
Victoria Cross, 9
War Office, British, 48, 53
Webb-Carter, Brian, 10, 13, 14
Whatley, Reg, 50
Wilson, G.B., 12

www.ingramcontent.com/pod-product-compliance
Lightning Source LLC
Chambersburg PA
CBHW040003080526
44586CB00027B/2871